Choose an Idea with Confidence!
Using the Start Up Safe Sequence

Written by Michael Timothy Allen Dip MRS

Dedication to

I dedicate this book to my amazing daughter and biggest hero I will ever know - Katia

Foreword

By Michael Timothy Allen

Firstly many thanks for buying my book.

42 percent of entrepreneurs blame lack of sales of their service or product for the failure of their business according to CB Insights in 2019.

Most people believe it is very difficult to find a good business idea, which you can scale and grow.

It can also be incredibly easy to jump into a venture and make the mistake of launching a flawed business idea, to an uninterested customer.

I wrote this book to help people avoid doing this.

Although we hear the failure builds entrepreneurial muscle, I take an opposing view. My earlier book Bouncepreneurs tries to help failed (yes failed) entrepreneurs bounce back from venture failure. Believe me it is not at all easy to do. In fact I will go further failure should be avoided at all costs!

I hate seeing good, hard working people fail at start up. I HATE IT I REALLY DO!

In our digital sharing world, credit rating can punish a family for a business failure for years. So I totally understand why many people are fearful of poor decisions. Even though they have the entrepreneurial bug, leaving the security of a well-paid job needs careful thought.

My goal is to be part of a movement that drives the 42 percent figure right down and with Choose an Idea with Confidence! I have set out a method for you.

I do not mind stating the obvious when I say care MUST be taken when choosing ideas. Vistaprint commissioned great piece of research in late 2018. It showed how 44 percent of UK, German, Italian and French entrepreneurs really cited the reason "products not solving the market's needs" as a top reason for failure.

In this book I will help even the most hesitant of entrepreneurs choose and confidently launch a successful start up. Choose an Idea with Confidence! is a street-wise, no nonsense approach, that will help hesitant and hasty entrepreneurs alike choose, research and test ideas. In this step-by-step guide, I will navigate you to find and use customer Pain Points as the basis of your start up.

I really have tried in this book to leave no stone unturned to protect your interests and guide you to success. You hard work and my Start Up Safe Sequence SUSS WILL give you the confidence to KNOW your idea WILL work on a full roll out. At the same time, you will be protecting you and your family from potential failure and costly damage to your wallet, confidence and time.

Should you wish to know more about my courses on Choose an Idea with Confidence! please visit www.chooseanidea.com where there is information. Also if you wish to access templates shown in this book in more usable formats please register on my site. Now go Choose an Idea with Confidence!

Table of Contents

Foreword

1. Introducing Choose an Idea

1.1. Welcome
1.2. There Are Too Many Start Ups Failing!
1.3. What You Will Learn
1.4. Old Way Doesn't Factor in Different Mind Sets
1.5. Flaws in the Old Way
1.6. Why I Want to Frighten You a Little Bit
1.7. The Choose an Idea Method
1.8. What you have learned in this chapter

2. Understanding Your Entrepreneurial Mind Set

2.1. What You Are Going to Learn in This Chapter
2.2. Take the Start Up Safe Sequence (SUSS) Mind Set Survey
2.3. The 4 Entrepreneurial Mind Sets
2.4. Moving Forward with Clearer Understanding of Your Mind Set
2.5. The Fox Mind Set

3. The Power of Pain Points in Choosing an Idea

3.1. What You Are Going to Learn in This Chapter
3.2. What is a Pain Point?
3.3. Triggers for Spotting Pain Points
3.4. The Six Types of Pain Points
3.5. Task
3.6. The 6 Types of Pain Points
3.7. What Are Wasting Time Pain Points?
3.8. What Are Wasting Money Pain Points?
3.9. What Are Crappy Tasks Pain Points?
3.10. What Are Lack of Support Pain Points?
3.11. What Are Embarassing Pain Points?
3.12. What Are Not Green Pain Points?
3.13 Your Task
3.14 What you have learned in this Chapter

4. The Start Up Safe Sequence SUSS Explained

4.1. What You Are Going to Learn in This Chapter
4.2. Understand Start Up Safe Sequence compare it to traditional approaches
4.3. Desert Mind Set Start Point
4.4. Tsunami Mind Start Point
4.5. Runaway Mind Start Point
4.6. Idol Mind Set Start Point
4.7 How the Professional Entrepreneur Fox Mind Set Does it?

4.8. It's Not All Ladders Going One Way
4.9. What you have learned in this Chapter

5. SUSS Idea Generation

5.1. What You Are Going to Learn in This Chapter
5.2. Using Life Experiences for Idea Generation
5.3. Top Tips for Effective Idea Generation
5.4. Brainwriting 635
5.5. Business Model Brainstorming (BMB)
5.6. Online Idea Generation
5.7. What you have learned in this Chapter

6. SUSS Idea Screening

6.1. What You Are Going to Learn in This Chapter
6.2. The Process Explained
6.3. Clarity
6.4. Alignment
6.5. Kooky
6.6. Evolution
6.8. Example A. IDEA SCREENING QUESTIONNAIRE
6.9. Example B. IDEA SCREENING QUESTIONNAIRE
6.10. Summary and Comparison Table for Your 10 Ideas
6.11. What you have learned in this Chapter

7. SUSS Market Research

7.1. What You Are Going to Learn in This Chapter
7.2. What are Information Targets?
7.3. Pain Point Information Target
7.4. Current Solution Information Target
7.5. Market Size Information Target
7.6. Spending Power Information Target
7.7. Demographics Information Target
7.8. Influencers Information Target
7.9. Location Information Target
7.10. Summary Plan
7.11. What you have learned in this Chapter

8. Start Up Safe Sequence Business Model

8.1. What You Are Going to Learn in this Chapter
8.2. Start Up Safe Sequence SuSS Canvas
8.3. Description – Pain Point
8.4. Description – Bankable Solution
8.5. Description – Single Target Customer
8.6. Description – Test Launch
8.7. Description – Key Partners
8.8. Description - Tribe

8.9. Description – Income 30/60/90
8.10. Description – Spend 30/60/90
8.11. Description – Key Tasks and Metrics
8.12. What you have learned in this Chapter

9. SUSS Test Launch - Minimum Viable Product Launch Explained

9.1. What You Are Going to Learn in This Chapter
9.2. MVP A Better Way
9.3. The 6 Launch Rules?
9.4. How to Build a MVP
9.5. Make Buying From You Easy
9.6. FAQ's
9.7. You Are Unable to Sell Your Product or Service – DROP
9.8 What if the Business Really Takes Off? – Ramp Up
9.9. What if there is demand but I see the need to change – PIVOT
9.10 What you have learned in this Chapter

10 SUSS Your Minimum Viable Product Mind Set

10.1 What You Are Going to Learn in This Chapter
10.2. Becoming an Accountant
10.3. Discovery
10.4. Voices of Doom and the Minefield of Expert Opinion
10.5. Be Intense
10.6. What exactly is Closing?
10.7. Energy is Key
10.8 What you have learned in this Chapter

11. SUSS Minimum Viable Product Effective Sales and Marketing

11.1 What You Are Going to Learn in This Chapter
11.2. Selling is the Primary Objective
11.3 No Need for the 7P's of Promotion – 3 are Simpler
11.4 Top 10 considerations in choosing your Launch Sales and Marketing plan
11.5. SUSS Sales and Marketing Launch Sheet Plan
11.7. Getting Leads
11.8. Converting
11.9. Delighting

12. Final Words and Tips

1. Introducing Choose an Idea

1.1. Welcome

Welcome to Choose an Idea from me Michael Allen your ally and guide.

Let me firstly congratulate you. Why? Because the very act of buying and opening this book tells that you are thinking about your new venture in an intelligent way.

I myself hate business failure. I HATE IT! That is why in my earlier book "Bouncepreneurs: Successfully Bounce Back After Business Failure," I showed failed entrepreneurs how to bounce back from failure. In my coaching work I have worked with many "failed entrepreneurs." I can tell you in this world of almost universal credit rating, failure IS something to be feared. It really is. Whilst it does offer significant learning experiences, the hardships of failure can be very brutal and too high a price to pay for the learning.

<u>So it is far better to learn to prevent failure when launching a new venture.</u>

In this book I seek to help four types of start up entrepreneur

- Those struggling to find a good idea for their start up
- Those with so many ideas they do not know which idea to choose
- Those who have an idea they almost worship and are blind to its potential weaknesses
- Those who have an idea and are racing to launch without enough testing

You will learn how your personal start up mind set works and how it can impact your potential for success. Typically all start up guides suggest one path <u>for all</u> mind sets. In Choose an Idea I show a more realistic and streetwise understanding of different entrepreneurial minds. The guidance I am offering provides a different approach dependant on your individual mind set.

1.2. There Are Too Many Start Ups Failing!

Whatever figure you have read about the proportion of businesses failing in their first year, we all know it is too high. Seriously high! This book has one simple goal to help reduce this percentage.

A statistic I read this year (2019), it really shocked me, was that 42 percent of start ups fail (in their first year) because <u>nobody wanted to buy</u> their product or service. Source: CB Insights 2019.

The Vistaprint Business Failure Study 2018

In October 2018 Vistaprint carried out a very important and insightful survey of entrepreneurs in the UK, France, Germany and Italy. A total of 2000 entrepreneurs were interviewed regarding business failure. The comments are my views by the way and not those of Vistaprint. Some of the key findings of that survey serve as a storm-warning to any entrepreneur preparing to dive into a new business without enough thought about their idea.

The Survey Said - 44 percent of entrepreneurs believe that having "a product that doesn't serve the market needs," to be a, or the major reason for business failure. In the UK the figure is 51 percent! **I Say** - Why not be certain you have a winner on your hands before diving into full launch.

The Survey Said - 67 percent of respondents said overcoming a business failure would be very or somewhat difficult. **I say** -So would it not be better to take all possible steps to avoid failure?

The Survey Said - If forced to close their business only 57 percent of entrepreneurs answered that they would consider opening a new one. **I Say** -Doesn't that suggest <u>real</u> pain is felt when you have to close down your business. Why suffer! There is no need for this to happen especially in year 1!

The Survey Said - Only 25 percent of entrepreneurs interviewed in the 2018 Vistaprint study agreed with the statement that "experiencing business failure was necessary to succeed." **I Say** - Now you are hearing it directly from real entrepreneurs. You do learn from failure, but it is not a prerequisite to success and it certainly should not be celebrated as a "must have" rite of passage.

The Survey Said - 39 percent of entrepreneurs admit that when they started their first business they had no idea of what they were doing. **I Say** – you do not have to be one of them!

The Survey Said - Entrepreneurs in the UK, Germany, France and Italy where asked what they could have done differently to succeed with earlier failed businesses. Understanding markets/being more strategic were the two most given answers. **I Say** – again it is all about market demand and strategy.

My Guarantee

Having read these statistics I set out to produce a book which will GUARANTEE a significant reduction in risk of failure and conversely increase your chances of success.

HOW? By making absolutely certain, that you Choose an Idea with confidence, you are personally aligned with AND give you the <u>maximum</u> chances of success. In this book you will be shown how to be CERTAIN customers want to buy your product or service BEFORE you commit serious cash (and typically a year of your life) to your start up.

I am assuming that readers are considering an idea or ideas. But if you are at a more advanced stage and already planning or about to launch an idea, this book will work for you too.

1.3. What You Will Learn

The most common thing failed entrepreneurs say when reviewing cause of 1st year failure is

"I wish I had tested my idea more thoroughly!"

In the Choose an Idea book you will learn to test thoroughly and increase your chance of success by:-

1. Understanding which of 4 Entrepreneurial Mind Sets you have
2. Following the Start Up Safe Sequence (SUSS) stage by stage process
3. Learn how to quickly and efficiently find and test ideas
4. Learn to use customer Pain Points as a compass to success

1.4. Old Way Doesn't Factor in Different Mind Sets

The old way of planning a business does not understand entrepreneurial thinking. Many entrepreneurs take short cuts, they skip market research altogether. You may be thinking of doing the same yourself! You won't be the first and you won't be the last, I assure you.

Often entrepreneurially-minded people simply cannot find the right idea nor have a flood of ideas. This changes the way they plan and execute their start up and can increase risk significantly.

For many entrepreneurs, once they are fixed on their "good idea" it will be launched come what may! Too often I am afraid it doesn't work out.

For the redundant man (concerned about paying the mortgage) that his idea to open an ornamental welding business may be poorly conceived; as he doesn't have a customer within 200 miles is like calling "his new born baby ugly." He will find it difficult to accept.

We all behave in different ways, but the good news is in the book you will find effective and well-meant safety nets to ensure you maximise your chances of success.

1.5. Flaws in the Old Way

If you follow the old way entrepreneurial process you will quickly see it is deeply flawed.

<u>Business planning does not link to idea generation</u>

Business planning does not link to idea generation. It comes much later (too late) in the process.

<u>Market research does not really prove buying intent</u>

Market research is good for some things, but it is highly deceiving when it comes to checking if customers will ACTUALLY buy your proposed product or service. I have suffered this myself, even after implementing a very good investigation.

<u>Too focused on offline research</u>

Our world is digital. The old way of finding out whether the market or individual customers exist uses surveys, focus groups and market information reports. They have their place, but there is so much more available to you than online reports and online questionnaires. Although a move forward, they are old methods on digital platforms. Do not misunderstand me, they definitely have a role to play for you, but there are many more, easy to use, digital methods available that need more airtime. We will give them airtime for you.

<u>Sequence of the process not fit for purpose</u>

The classic sequence of testing a market for customer demand is actually not fit for purpose.

Why?

Because it does not run in a straight line or allow back tracking if an idea proves too weak to take to market.

<u>Not all entrepreneurs are the same</u>

Firstly it does nothing to understand some entrepreneurs have one dominant idea, others none and some too many. So starting with generating new ideas is only the start point for one or (at a stretch) two of the four types of start up entrepreneur.

If you are the entrepreneur with a single idea, most likely you will go straight through screening ideas (as you'll only care about one!) to market research. Because you only have one idea you'll likely skip or ignore the research anyway and jump feet first into full blown expensive launch.

If on the other hand, you are the entrepreneur with too many ideas, you will not know which of your ideas really hits customer demand. Why? Because you simply cannot take 20 ideas into market research. But if you can be encouraged to reduce the number of ideas before you do detailed market research on pain points, you will be more successful.

Lastly, if you are the willing entrepreneur short of ideas the old way sequence, also does not work. You are generating ideas abstract from any sense of direction or personal alignment.

<u>Slow and academic</u>

The reason so many start up entrepreneurs (and bigger businesses) go recklessly from idea to launch, without doing much research, is because they perceive the process as slow, energy draining and expensive. I some cases they believe they just know better!

Although it is improving, many of the start up guides you get from many government agencies, banks and accountants are well meaning but very academic and stuffy. They mean well, but too often they push hard for risky innovation and introduction of venture capital.

1.6. Why I Want to Frighten You a Little Bit

I am passionate about protecting entrepreneurs from failure. I really am. So forgive these tough words. I would rather be the lone voice of caution before you invest your energy and savings than one of the many "Told You So" after the business does not work out.

In my work I have taken many clients through the classic OLD WAY process of idea generation – market research – launch. But the truth is for the individual entrepreneur it is not straightforward and for this reason they bypass much of it, significantly increasing their risk of failure.

But simply put, the old way of finding ideas and launching new businesses is plain dangerous to your long term

- Finances
- Family and
- Mental Health

The danger of big stuffy business plans, borrowing and having advisors who might as well be speaking Klingon – it not just tired and ineffective – it is dangerous!

The standard methods of start up planning are simply not protecting entrepreneurs like you from failure. Start up planning is extremely frivolous and failure is extremely serious. Behind every person in the statistics is a family or individual often in difficulty or crisis.

Once again we have 42 percent of start ups failing (CB Insight 2019) due to no demand for their product! Similar people to you, not fools, intelligent, driven and hard working. But they still failed!

Do you really want to be in the 4 in 10?

Of course you don't. Plus there are other reasons why your business might fail. But demand really does not have to be one of them.

So beware, there is a huge machine out there (in the public and private sector) encouraging everyone to spend on starting their own business. I do mean everybody – women, ethnic minorities, kids, retired, redundant, ex-military, older male offenders are all being specifically targeted to start their own business. Perhaps you have seen this yourself.

Everyone wants to be around when the champagne corks are popping and the cameras are clicking, when you open your business. But as I have learned by running the Bouncepreneurs programme if you launch a small business and fail these days you can **really** struggle afterwards. Quite honestly I think it was better for the Victorians in some ways!

More and more people are experiencing a new form of discrimination after venture failure. The old idea that if your business fails, you simply get a job is a DEEPLY FLAWED assumption. Modern day credit rating can seriously damage your ability to secure a job after business failure. I personally think it has become a form of discrimination on the same level as race, sexuality and age.

Collectively we do see that business failure IS something to be feared. Sure you do learn, of course you do. But the impact of failure can be very painful for years.

It is not surprising that in the areas of real economic distress, where jobs are very hard to get, the interest in starting a small business in some disadvantaged communities is actually falling, because of Fear of Failure.

Finally, encouraging entrepreneurship is something I applaud. If it is done right!

1.7. The Choose an Idea Method

I will guide you to significantly increase your chances of launch success.

You will fully understand your own Mind Set type (Chapter 2) and adjust your approach for greater success.

You will have total focus on Pain Points! Chapter 3 explains Pain Points in depth.

You will follow the Start Up Safe Sequence or SUSS for short. This is a clear stage by stage process that you can go up and down and this is explained in Chapter 4.

Together, Mind Set, Pain Points and SUSS will empower you to success.

This will give you more confidence because the process is much simpler to understand and implement than conventional approaches.

You'll be encouraged to fully test your idea, on a very light and inexpensive basis. Rather than skipping the process you will keep it very simple. This will massively reduce your risk of failure.

If you ask any sales coach, what she trains her sales people to spot in conversation with prospects – it is pain points! So all we are really doing is lifting a proven concept from success in sales and making it your compass for idea evaluation.

Because Pain Points are so important to your success I will always use capital P's when referring to them! Pain Points.

Understanding Mind Sets of Entrepreneurs

I understand that you entrepreneurs approach choosing, testing and launching ideas in different ways. So I have come up with 4 types of mind set amongst start up entrepreneurs. This allows me to encourage all entrepreneurs in different ways and motivate you to "measure twice and cut once," on your ideas.

By encouraging you to think about your approach to your business ideas, testing and launch, you benefit from risk reduction. Those of you charging forward may need a "friendly prod with a Taser" to slow down and look around a little more. Some of you desperate to be self-employed, but struggle for that single amazing idea. You need encouragement, rather than made to feel uncreative.

My approach is asking you to recognise your strengths and weaknesses so they are positive and not destructive in your ramp up to business launch.

Common theme and thread through all process stages

By making your whole process of researching choosing and launching focus on the concept of customer Pain Points, you will find a Safer Start up. You will reduce the risk of failure very significantly and have far greater confidence in the idea.

Your search for and refinement of a Pain Point that will hold you on course for success.

You will also be able to speak a common language to others reading this book or taking the course, enabling you to learn collectively.

Integrates online and offline research

You will be shown a very specific shopping list of information that you need to collect and use in your search for Pain Points. I will make this process easier for you.

You will have a more up-to-date approach to online research, going further than simply searching Google or sourcing research reports.

You need to have enough accessible customers to build a scalable and repeatable business. So you will be shown how to quantify the market opportunity for the Pain Point you have discovered.

You will build a customer profile from your idea and research – starting with the Pain Point and building to a full understanding of your customer in the form of an ideal customer Avatar profile. The exact type of people you are after as customers.

Streamlines the process

This approach is simpler than the old way.

We spell out the stages of the process right from the beginning, so you are in no doubt what you need to do to follow the process successfully.

You will also be more precise in the information you need to find and the surveys you need to construct. You will also be confident in designing your customer and expert interviews. This means less work and faster progress.

Fast

This process is faster than the Old Way because you will find it

1. Clearer – with simple instructions at every stage
2. More logical to the start up entrepreneur
3. More streetwise and free of jargon
4. You get templates questionnaires to reduce your workload

1.8. What you have learned in this chapter

At the beginning and every Chapter I summarise the main things you are learning.

In this Chapter you have discovered my philosophy toward business failure and why I am driven to reduce failure rates amongst start ups.

You will have heard why the Old Way of choosing and lunching a business is now obsolete and that there is a much safer way.

You have heard the terms Pain Points, Start Up Safe Sequence and Mind Sets. Now let's learn more about your Mind Set in Chapter 2.

2. Understanding Your Entrepreneurial Mind Set

2.1. What You Are Going to Learn in This Chapter

In this Chapter you will see the importance of understanding your own MIND SET and how it impacts your ability to Choose an Idea. You will also see how your Mind Set affects your chances of success. If you search online or read business books about start ups you see reasons for success and failure.

You will read "the business succeeded for these reasons," see

- Funding
- Business Model
- Ideas
- Team
- Timing

Or "the business failed for these reasons,"

- No market need
- Ran out of cash
- Not the right team
- Get out competed
- Pricing/cost issues

Now these are intelligent observations without a doubt. BUT what is not discussed is

The Mind Set of the start up entrepreneur.

I believe the mind set of every entrepreneur to be different in regards to their start up. Here are some of the influences that affect it. The 10 P's. Which of these do you associate with:-

1. Pressures to pay bills as soon as possible
2. Patience levels in doing the research process on ideas
3. Peer pressure from others to sell certain products or just to get started
4. Previous failures, which increase fear of failure
5. Personality in general, some people are of course always in a rush, some take their time
6. Proficiency in generating ideas, many entrepreneurs really struggle to come up with ideas
7. Persistence with a single idea
8. Perception of the difference between a start up as a job or scalable business
9. Persuadable by facts or not persuadable by facts
10. Pain points and understanding what they really are

You will learn to better understand your own Mind Set and the Mind Sets of other entrepreneur types which will give you much greater clarity of thought when Choosing an Idea. You may start to become less emotionally attached to any existing ideas. You will see where your Mind Set typically starts their Choose an Idea journey and decide if this is really the best route for you.

2.2. Take the Start Up Safe Sequence (SUSS) Mind Set Survey

Welcome to the SUSS Mind Set Survey where you will discover which of the four entrepreneur mind sets you currently have. There are no right or wrong answers and no trick questions. So relax, you will not end up in Slytherin House at Hogwarts! Although it is realistic! Simply select the answer A, B, C or D that best applies to you. Just one answer please.

Q1. How much pressure to pay urgent bills are you under at the moment?		
Which best describes you. Select just one option with a single X	X	Office Use Only
Very serious pressure, I cannot sleep		A
Some pressure		C
I do not have to worry I have it covered		D
I am not worried at all, plenty of money to cover bills		B

Q2. How much patience do you have for doing research on your businesses ideas		
Which best describes you. Select just one option with a single X	X	Office Use Only
I find it difficult to be patient as I have a great idea already		B
I will spend as long as it takes getting to the right idea		D
I have no time to be doing this		A
If only I had an idea to research		C

Q3. Do you feel peer pressure from others to sell certain products or just to get started		
Which best describes you. Select just one option with a single X	X	Office Use Only
A friend or colleague introduced me to a product I can sell		A
There is no pressure but the idea I have is a winner		B
No there is no real pressure on me		D
The only pressure on me is to find a good idea		C

Q4. Have you previously failed in business or in a job, does this make you frightened of failing?		
Which best describes you. Select just one option with a single X	X	Office Use Only
I have no fear of failure, because my idea will work		B
I have failed before and this makes it difficult to commit to an idea		C
The most important thing is to get my idea in the market while it's fresh		A
I am not worried, if this idea fails I have plenty more in my head		D

Q5. What sort of personality do you have? Pick the description you feel describes you best		
Which best describes you. Select just one option with a single X	X	Office Use Only
Carpe diem! – seize the day is my motto		A
I don't care what the crowd thinks – I back my own judgement every time		B
Sometimes I struggle to make big decisions		C
I am a highly creative thinker and problem solver		D

Q6. How good do you think you are at coming up with business ideas?

Which best describes you. Select just one option with a single X	X	Office Use Only
I am really good at spotting winning ideas		B
I am ok, but I have a friend who is very helpful		A
If anything I am too good at coming up with ideas		D
This is something I really struggle with		C

Q7. How do you rate the likely success of your current idea?

Which best describes you. Select just one option with a single X	X	Office Use Only
The idea I have now is certain to succeed		B
The evidence from the people who gave me this idea gives me confidence		A
Which idea are we talking about I have several great ideas		D
I do not have a strong idea at the moment		A

Q8. What do you think about the scale of the business you plan to create?

Which best describes you. Select just one option with a single X	X	Office Use Only
So long as I can create an idea to provide a wage I am happy		A
I want to take the great idea I have to the stars		B
I understand scalability and this makes it harder to find a good idea		C
Some of my ideas are just jobs and some can grow big		D

Q9. Persuadable by facts?

Which best describes you. Select just one option with a single X	X	Office Use Only
My own judgement is better than all other facts given to me		B
I pay attention to the facts given to me by my prospective business partners		A
Sometimes a quick good plan is better than a slow certain one		D
Absolute certainty in facts drive what I do in entrepreneurship		C

Q10. Pain points and what they really are?

Which best describes you. Select just one option with a single X	X	Office Use Only
I understand pain points, my elbow has them every winter		A
I see lots of opportunities out there, customer pain points are everywhere		D
I haven't spotted a strong pain point anywhere		C
My product addresses a real pain point without doubt		B

Now once you have completed the survey, look at the "Office Use Only" column. Count how many A's, B's, C's or D's you have. Now pick the highest scoring letter. That is your dominant mind set in start up. Now let us set what that means. Take a look at the following page.

2.3. The 4 Entrepreneurial Mind Sets

Here are the four mind sets of typical entrepreneurs. This applies to those at start up, people who run other businesses AND people working inside major businesses too. The letter you have scored most highly on is your Mind Set type. If you score equally, then you are a combination of the 2 types.

The four Mind Sets are

- A. Runaway
- B. Idol
- C. Desert
- D. Tsunami

So your start up Mind Set is most closely linked to one of these characterisations. Do remember none of these Mind Sets are better or worse than the others. But you will benefit by understanding all four. Do not worry; I will explain each one in detail for you.

runaway

Summary: Like the runaway express train this type of entrepreneur only wants to get to their destination, which is to launch their idea into the market.

Drivers for Runaway types

- Commonly accept on face value business ideas from other people. They are especially receptive to franchise businesses, multi-level marketing or working as distributors/extensions of friend's or relative's businesses.
- Runaways are often pushed by people into a certain type of business; they can even be susceptible to bullying.
- Their haste is sometimes due to real financial problems and the need to do something to save the family home.
- Their behaviour can be frantic
- They will often start a business in a market they do not know AND need to use a skill that is new to them at the same time

Attitude towards market investigation

The Runaway cannot entertain spending time investigating the market they plan to serve.

Their yardstick is whether someone else is making money in that field. So they study competitive products closely.

They rarely investigate service models, or the role service has in the customers buying decisions.

Launch Marketing and Sale

Traditional, face to face or telephone sales is the marketing method of choice for this individual. Runaways are not big on social media (the Runaways that do succeed are good at digital marketing); often they are very hard-working and driven to get the business off the ground.

But they can exhaust themselves physically and financially for little real return. Runaways NEVER test launch, it is always straight in to full blown launch investment.

idol

Summary: The Idol entrepreneur treats their single idea like a golden child idol. They will not allow criticism of it from anyone. They have a strong, but sometimes blind faith.

Drivers for Idol types

- Idol types have a sincere and deeply held view that their product or service is a winner.
- There are some very successful entrepreneurs out there who held their ideas before them like Idols and were successful. Henry Ford was a good example and is thought to have said "if I had listened I would have given them faster horses." But they are exceptions.
- Many entrepreneurs of the Idol variety are inventors and coders. They have an idea and believe in it with every cell in their body.
- The problem is that for every Idol type who is a success there are dozens that fail.
- The most concerning thing about Idols is there inability to see when an idea is not going to work OR indeed clearly is not working. They will push on for years believing the market will come around to their way of thinking.
- Idols are fiercely defensive of criticism and turn nasty if their reasoning is questioned.

Attitude towards market investigation

Unlike the Runaway the Idol will do market research. They are very happy if it shows they are correct and will use the research effectively to build up their launch.

But if the research shows the Idol's idea to be weak in any way, or even not fit to launch, they will ignore, belittle or generally try to disrespect the methodology or source behind the research.

Idols will not accept any criticism of their idea.

Launch Marketing and Sales

Idols rarely test launch. If they do and use market research, they will only take notice of it, if it supports their viewpoint. If it shows results critical to the idea, they will totally ignore it.

Idols are very good bloggers. In sales roles they TELL rather than LISTEN to customers. Many are trapped in poverty for years trying to launch their idea and refuse to accept defeat.

desert

Summary: The Desert entrepreneur struggles with ideas. They are more common than you think. People who really want, or claim to want to be entrepreneurs but simply cannot come up with ideas.

Drivers for Idol types

- The Desert type entrepreneur is often paralysed by fear of failure. They just do not want to fail and set a very high standard for ideas, which in the real world can never be attained.
- Desert types are very often comfortable in highly paid jobs. They work for very large businesses, live in major cities and earn large salaries.
- Because this type has a high disposable income, they are notably interested in very highly performing and very SAFE bets. Why else would they give up their own secure job?
- Desert types like venture capital, crowdsourcing and investors. They are more comfortable investing other peoples' money rather than their own.
- Deserts struggle to commit to ideas. They think like the major enterprises they work for. This can lead to over-thinking, resulting in paralysing detail and frequent discarding of ideas.
- Desert entrepreneurs can be more interested in entrepreneurship as a fashion trend than the real business work, enjoying mixing with entrepreneurs more than becoming one.

Attitude towards market investigation

The Deserts will research ideas very well, if they are given the idea by a team member or partner. They love the process of critiquing ideas and often dismiss perfectly good ideas rather than risk a commercial launch.

Launch Marketing and Sales

Deserts can be extremely good at assessing test launches. They are strong note takers and spread sheet analysers! But the simple truth is they rarely get to the launch stage.

Often this individual will be extremely good at digital marketing and does the best of all types in social media based product promotions.

tsunami

Summary: A brainstorming session with the Tsunami type entrepreneur will sweep you away by sheer volume of their ideas. They struggle to settle on any one long enough to see it to launch.

Drivers for Idol types

- Tsunami are very creative and very dynamic idea generators
- Failure does not faze them. In fact they can be very reckless.
- As Richard Branson is reputed to say "Ideas are like buses, if you miss one, there will be another one along in a minute." The trouble is with Tsunami types they jump from idea to idea without ever leaving the idea generation phase.
- When they do settle on a single idea, it is normally a good one. But they will always want to extend the range, add colours or diversify into another market, often without cementing the core revenue of the start up
- Often very engaging, helpful and generous people

Attitude towards market investigation

Getting the Tsunami to migrate from idea generation to research investigation can be difficult. But when they apply their energy to research it is often fantastic work. No stone will be left unturned with the Tsunami entrepreneur.

Tsunamis are very afraid of failure too. They often seek to swap out their current idea from launch at the last minute with a better alternative. This is driven by fear.

Launch Marketing and Sales

Tsunami entrepreneurs are afraid of selling. They are more comfortable finding new ideas than selling or marketing them. Tsunami's find routine boring

However, if they do launch successfully they are superb at customer service and often highly creative in improving customer experience. If a Tsunami comprehends service can be more important than product they are powerful entrepreneurs.

2.4. Moving Forward with Clearer Understanding of Your Mind Set

You have seen which of the 4 characterisations you are most aligned with. Each of the 4 types has flaws, but also strengths too. Here we show the start up process we suggest for each Mind Set type.

A Flexible Approach to Ideas and Launch Based on Your Mind Set	
Mind Set	**Most Suitable Way to Progress**
runaway	The Runaway is the express train when it comes to ideas. Normally you pick up a single idea very quickly and race to launch with nothing in between. A Safer Start Up for Runaways is to carry out a compact study to see if the Idea is hitting real customer pain points. Then to see if the business model is really in your interests.
idol	The Idol is the most stubborn of the 4 types and you do not really listen to negative market research. No matter how hard you are persuaded it is a "NO", you want to launch now. A Safer Start Up for those Idols amongst you is to go to launch, but a Test launch, where your money and time is minimised. If it fails it is a fast fail and you can come back to fresh idea generation, without losing too much time, money and energy.
desert	There are more Desert entrepreneurs than any other category. You want a great idea, but struggle on the idea generation. Once you get some good ideas you will do just great. A Safer Start Up for you is Idea Generation, Screening, Business Model, Test Launch and Launch. A classic path to success. Well supported and clear instructions all the way.
tsunami	Tsunamis have no problems with ideas, but a challenge sticking with one. By carrying out a full Screening process on your many ideas, we can increase your confidence in your selection and reduce your fear of failure. Further testing in market research and test launch will set your mind at ease.

2.5. The Fox Mind Set

I would like to introduce the Fox Mind Set. We all know how foxes are thought to be amongst the most cunning and clever of animals. But it is not why I choose the fox to represent the best traits of an entrepreneur seeking a Safer Start Up.

fox

The real reason is their power to **identify opportunity** and **adapt**. Yes identify opportunity and then adapt to different circumstances. They have adapted to opportunities and there are many varieties. Did you know there are Bat-eared foxes, tiny Fennec foxes, Grey Foxes, Red Ones, White Artic Foxes; the Ethiopian wolf is a fox. There are Pampas foxes, Darwin's foxes and even a Crab-eating fox.

Be like a fox identify opportunity and adapt!

The **two** most important traits of a Safer Start Up are

Being able to **identify opportunity** AND that means being able to spot real customer **PAIN POINTS**

Being able to **adapt** AND that means putting pursuit of clearly verifiable customer **PAIN POINTS** above any pre-conceptions, pride or pet projects.

2.6. What you have learned in this chapter

In this Chapter you have seen that entrepreneurs have different Mind Sets. These are driven by personality and life experiences. All types have strengths and weaknesses. But the main learning is about balancing emotional attachment to any idea with objective thinking.

In the next Chapter you will learn about more about PAIN POINTS as a way of finding great ideas.

3. The Power of Pain Points in Choosing an Idea

3.1. What You Are Going to Learn in This Chapter

In this Chapter I will raise your understanding of PAIN POINTS and show you how customer pain points are the COMPASS to success in finding great business ideas.

What is a Pain Point? A Pain Point is something that gives a customer real pain in their life OR business. It is something they really would prefer to be without. They are not the same for everyone.

If you can find a **real** Pain Point, which you have the resources to serve you will do very well. Why? Because once you identify a Pain Point, you have found an idea that customers and businesses will pay to make disappear. If you can show that you can make it go away, they will spend with you and maybe they will keep spending. When they keep spending this is called being a "sticky" product.

There are 6 customer Pain Points. You'll be learning to spot them all in this Chapter.

1. Wasting precious time
2. Spending too much money
3. Having to do frustrating or unpleasant tasks (crappy tasks)
4. Not getting expected support
5. Dealing with highly embarrassing/personal problems (embarrassing)
6. Having to throw things away when trying to be green (not green)

3.2. What is a Pain Point?

A pain point is something that gives a customer real pain in their life OR business. It is something they really would prefer to be without.

Sometimes a customer may have a small degree of discomfort that is not enough to make them buy, change behaviour or switch supplier. But a true pain point would.

A great way of explaining a true pain point is comparing a customer buying a vitamin to prevent further decay of their joints. Compared to them buying painkillers because the pain is in their hip joint has stopped them sleeping for six months.

If this customer were to face greater pressure on their finances they would stop buying the vitamins, but keep buying the pain killers.

There are several types of Pain Points. Four are commonly cited. But I have 6 Pain Points for you.

1. Wasting precious time
2. Spending too much money
3. Having to do frustrating or unpleasant tasks (crappy tasks)
4. Not getting expected support
5. Dealing with highly embarrassing/personal problems (embarrassing)
6. Having to throw things away when trying to be green (not green)

You will get to know these better later on.

3.3. Triggers for Spotting Pain Points

The Runaways, Tsunamis and Idols among you will already have one or more ideas. But what actually has triggered your idea in the first place? One of these problem Pain Points perhaps?

- Something you have experienced personally
- A problem somebody told you they had experienced
- A problem you have witnessed happening to someone else – maybe your children or relatives
- A strong solution to a problem you have never seen in your country, but commonly used in another land.
- A problem you have seen causing Pain in your place of work
- A problem that you have seen in research, article or study

We all know Spiderman, remember his "Spidey Sense" for danger. Well you can develop a Pain Point Sense. Just by thinking about the triggers above your mind will start to identify more Pain Points.

You will start to observe problems at home or your children/parents/friends/colleagues have. Start to ask friends to explain more about their problems, at home or at their work.

Start looking for real Pain Points. A business based on a real Pain Point is far more likely to succeed and they make for much Safer Start Ups.

3.4. The Six Types of Pain Points

On the page below you will see the six Pain Points as images. On the next six pages we look at each of them in more detail.

You will see a more expansive description of what each of the Pain Points is. I also provide examples and commentary on each one in turn.

<u>Vitamins versus Pain Killers</u>

We use the great term Vitamins versus Pain Killers to encourage you to think about the scale of pain being felt in the examples. When you are assessing your own ideas you can think about this too.

This is all about the process of discovering Pain Points and making you more receptive to what you are hearing, seeing and experiencing.

While you are reading these I would like you to consider:-

- It is only a true Pain Point if you really feel some pain!
- If it is a true Pain Point and it is not resolved it should lead to a big problem or crisis
- Timing alone can create Pain Points
- Some Pain Points are socially unacceptable and companies who choose to ignore them will feel the anger of staff and customers alike
- Green and environmental momentum is building into a revolution. There are many Pain Points in this market to base business ideas on

3.5. Task

As you go through the 6 Types of Pain Points, think of a pain point that you have seen that fits the type. It does not have to be one of your business ideas. But of course, you can use one if you choose.

Write it down on the page after the 6 Types. Give it a name. Describe it in a sentence or two.

Then think about whether it is a Vitamin or a Pain Killer Medicine.

We have a page after the six Pain Point descriptions for you. It is shown after the 6 Types are shown. There is a scale which you can score the Pain Point on.

1 is a Vitamin and Not a Strong Pain Point. 5 is a very strong Pain Point. Put a circle around the most appropriate number 1 2 3 4 or 5.

It is task to get you thinking about multiple types of Pain Points and not just one or two.

3.6. The 6 Types of Pain Points

3.7. What Are Wasting Time Pain Points?

Wasting Time Pain Points are not simply about time on a watch or clock. Although they can be time based. They could be 30 seconds here or 10 minutes there.

But they can also be:-

- Not seeing your children after school, because you get home too late from work
- Business time wasters like sales prospects that waste your time and have no serious intent to buy from you.
- Time wasting in a mechanical, refining or other industrial process.
- There are community time wasters too, such as wasting time filling up the old diesel generator creating power for your remote village. Or walking miles to collect water.
- It could be a relationship also. This can be a huge cause of pain and staying in it may be considered by some wasted years. Again time.

Example

Marcus di Maria a brilliant British educator on stock or share trading is in great physical shape too. He surprised me by saying he thought going to the gym wasted time!

Yes going to the gym! If it is a 20 minute trip each way, that is 40 minutes wasted. Now if you had a home gym you could do your workout in the morning and get it done as part of your routine, saving 40 minutes each time.

Vitamin versus Pain Killer Medicine

Assume your business sold home gyms. Would your offering represent a vitamin or a pain killer? Many gym goers go to see friends and social aspects. For them saving the time is not a pain killer. It may not even be a vitamin.

But for the busy time-poor parent who struggles to find time to go to the gym, it's **certainly** a vitamin. But if the same person has been told to lose weight by their doctor and they are a pre-diabetic, then it **is** a pain killer.

3.8. What Are Wasting Money Pain Points?

Whether it is in business or in the home wasting money is a cause of Pain Points.

- Not understanding money, not understanding how to stop wasting it, is in itself a Pain Point.
- Homes and especially mortgages are a Pain Point for many people. Not just those who have fallen into arrears, but those with 25 years of payments ahead of them. This leads into another Pain Point, that of trust. People often know they are wasting money but do not know whose advice to trust.
- Food waste is nowadays such a hot topic that there are several TV shows about it. It is a clear financial and ethical Pain Point for most people.
- In business, wasting money Pain Points are often in open view. One of the biggest wastes of money is losing valuable talent, especially programmers and qualified trade labour.
- Another big waste of money is running a sales team that is not selling enough. Businesses will listen to those who can solve this Pain Point.
- Unused software subscriptions cost businesses millions. It is a real waste of money and therefore Pain Point where a solution will be rewarded.
- Wasting expensive energy is the most obvious of Pain Points in terms of wasting money. Especially in heavy manufacturing processes like steel making. But also, of course, in the home.

Example

Jo travels to work daily. It is a 20 minute drive in her car. Sam her neighbour works in the same supermarket. They could commute together and share the fuel bill.

Vitamin versus Pain Killer Medicine

Now if Jo is really struggling making ends meet, the idea of car sharing to save money is very attractive and a Pain Killer. For Sam her drive is used to call her elderly mother and check if she is ok.

Saving on travel, would help Jo as a Pain Killer Medicine saving. But for Sam it stops her checking in and running errands for her mother. So car sharing for Sam is not a Pain Killer Medicine and not really even a Vitamin. Two people, similar situations, different Pain Points. Remember this!

crappy tasks

3.9. What Are Crappy Tasks Pain Points?

Crappy tasks are everywhere. They are in your home, your job, in your club, your place of worship and of course in companies and government agencies. It helps if you think of dirty tasks. Crappy tasks are also linked to wasting time of course, but it is the unpleasantness of them that counts. People will moan about them and often moan loud and clear, they are actually quite easy to spot.

Examples

- Clearing vermin such as persistent rats or removing a wasps nest
- Taking daily injections (literally a Pain Point)
- Removing asbestos or other hazardous waste
- Entering monotonous forms
- Customising CV's for many different job adverts
- Serving angry clients all day long
- Keeping driveways weed free or clearing brambles

Vitamin versus Pain Killer Medicine

Many clubs and societies have uniforms. Not just sports kit but choirs also buy uniforms. A local triathlon club had branded kit for members including hoodies, T Shirts, race suits and swimming trunks. Wearing the club colours on race day, as well as training sessions was important to members. But ordering it was not easy. Not easy at all. Sometimes it took 6 months to get a race suit.

It is a familiar story to many, I think! The club administrator disliked managing the ordering, but hated the returns process. She kept telling the leadership about it, over and over again.

Now to the administrator the kit issue was a Pain Killer issue. But for years the club leadership saw it as a Vitamin issue. Only when the administrator resigned and members started to leave in favour of a rival club, citing problems with getting kit as a major reason did it become a Pain Killer issue to the leaders.

Failing to solve the Pain Point led to a crisis.

lack of support

3.10. What Are Lack of Support Pain Points?

Lack of support Pain Points offer lots of opportunities for entrepreneurs. There are many customers out there – both consumers and businesses that are feeling unloved by their current suppliers.

- Unable to get ANY support – when customers cannot get any support it is a massive Pain Point. Find an organisation doing this and that has a product you can match, then you have a great idea opportunity.
- Selfish support – this is when the support offered by the organisation is by design suited to the needs of the organisation and not the client. When AO.com started to offer hourly delivery slots for kitchen appliances, they broke the selfish approach of the big UK retailers. By 2012 with AO growing rapidly Comet the UK's second biggest electrical retailer failed closing over 200 stores.
- Support too complex – if customers do not understand support it's a Pain Point.
- Unfriendly – if clients are consistently or repeatedly treated in an unfriendly manner, they are receptive to change providers.
- On the wrong channel – force someone without a Smartphone to be supported online, they will feel pain and call an alternative supplier from their house phone! The opportunity is being the alternative supplier.
- Poor quality of service solution – if the actual solution offered by the supplier to fix the problem goes wrong or does not work repeatedly, there is an opportunity to capitalise on this Pain Point.

Example

Stephen and Tracey bought a hot tub for their garden. The family loved it and it was used regularly by them and guests at their many barbeques. After a few years the cover needing replacement. The original tub supplier offered a replacement that took 6 weeks to arrive! It was peak hot tub season.

Vitamin versus Pain Killer Medicine

A clear Pain Killer example! Without the cover the tub was unuseable. Stephen and Tracey wanted that cover, had the money to buy it and were not going to wait 6 weeks. Opportunity knocks!

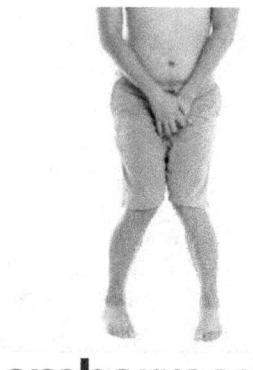

embarrassing

3.11. What Are Embarassing Pain Points?

This in my view is the biggest of the untapped Pain Points. Embarrassment is a gigantic industry. From buying condoms over the counter, to asking for Viagra or for both men and women dealing with hair loss. Embarrassment is the Godzilla of Pain Points. Take away embarrassment, guilt or shame with a worthy product or service, then customers will love you for it.

- Things people do not want to buy over the counter are many. Head lice shampoo, condoms, wart remover, pregnancy test kits, incontinence pants, anti-fungal powder are just a few examples. Offer a credible solution you can deliver by post then you solve a Pain Point.
- Cars are a huge Pain Point to some people. A more desirable vehicle can really solve a Pain Point.
- Sex products are an embarrassing Pain Point. Not everyone can go shopping in Amsterdam.
- Businesses cannot afford the embarrassment of offensive or inappropriate speech by employees in social media or company spaces physical and online. It creates a clear Pain Point.
- Companies have been fined in court for allowing management to turn a blind eye to individuals bullying, being racist, sexist or predatory to colleagues. These are now big financial penalties. Embarrassing Pain Points really affecting leadership teams and even share prices.
- Loss of data and hacking are also embarrassing Pain Points. It does not just affect global businesses. Any idea that help to tackle these problems will get a hearing within businesses now.

Example

A large telecom business had a predatory sales manager known for harrassing females in his team. His behaviour was accepted and condoned by many colleagues. He posted inappropriate comments about a female colleague and circulated them to colleagues and some customers.

Vitamin versus Pain Killer Medicine

The management knew it to be a time bomb. A definite Pain Point. They would be receptive to a service offering cultural training for the sales team and a service to monitor social media and email for offensive material.

not green

3.12. What Are Not Green Pain Points?

Consumers are beginning to vote with their wallets and put real pressure on global companies and governments to change. But consumers (especially younger consumers) feel Pain Points when they throw away needlessly, and avoid this by buying differently.

Throwing away plastic bottles - Consumers are increasingly uncomfortable with plastic waste. They often actually physically see a bag full of plastic bottles being dumped every week. So it is a regularly felt pain point. Ideas to tackle this will thrive.

Kids see the turtle having a plastic drinking straw pulled out of it's nostril, they see the impact of plastic on our seas. Children really feel this Pain Point and tell their parents they <u>must not</u> buy plastic straws. That creates real opportunity for alternatives.

In the Netherlands you can return glass bottles and jars to machines outside the supermarket you bought them from, getting a discount. A Pain Point successfully reduced.

In businesses more and more companies look to source post consumer waste paper, products and packaging. It is a Pain Point for staff <u>not</u> to recycle at work.

Companies feel pain if the do not understand the direction that consumers are taking with green buying behaviour. It is a Pain Point from them if competitors successfully launch green alternatives.

A company with a history of environmental damage cannot hide from it anymore. This Pain Point is best countered with cause marketing which you may be able to help with as a PR agency.

Example

The plastic razor is one of the oldest disposable products. Everytime I have to use one I personally felt guilty. The fancier they are the more pain I feel.

Vitamin versus Pain Killer Medicine

Did I need a Vitamin or Pain Killer Medicine. It has become a Pain Point so I bought a single blade safety razor and a vintage strop machine. I now use soap and a shaving brush (non badger), showing Pain Points cause change in markets. More importantly they create opportunity for you!

3.13 Your Task – Write a description for each Pain Point and circle how strong a Pain Point you think it is Score it 1 = Vitamin 5 Pain Killer. Think about Pain Points you've seen or experienced.

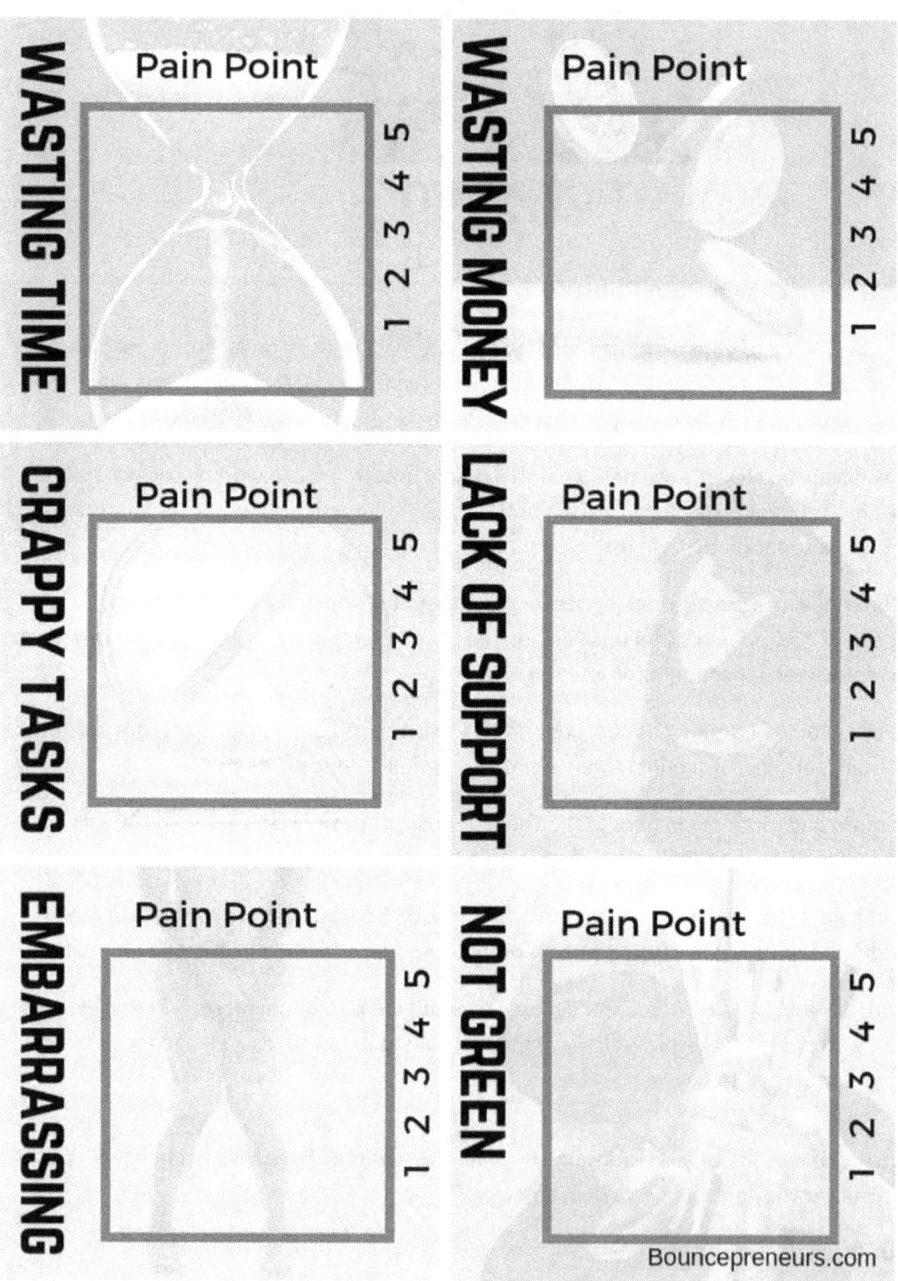

Bouncepreneurs.com

3.14 What you have learned in this Chapter

In this Chapter you have learned all about Pain Points. You have seen the different types and what gives rise to them.

We've also looked at the difference between minor and major Pain Points which we've called Vitamin and Pain Killer types.

You now know that finding and solving Pain Killer type Pain Points is a really great way to guide you towards Choosing an Idea. Not just any idea, but a great idea!

In the next Chapter you will learn all about the Start Up Safe Sequence – your road map to blending your search for a great idea with a lower risk Safer Start Up.

4. The Start Up Safe Sequence SUSS Explained

4.1. What You Are Going to Learn in This Chapter

What you will learn in this Chapter is the Start Up Safe Sequence or SUSS for short. You will be shown where to jump into the SUSS based on your Mind Set type. There explanations for each Mind Set further down in this Chapter. They are specifically for you, WHERE to jump into the development of your idea at the best stage for YOU. You will also see how the Professional Entrepreneur – the Fox does it.

Now conventional wisdom suggests that ALL start ups and company product development should go through a uniform idea creation to launch process. But my work with many start-ups over the years has shown that most entrepreneurs will do it their own way come what may.

So the way my method works is to EXPECT entrepreneurs like you to jump into the start up process at different stages, depending on circumstances and their type.

- Idol
- Desert
- Tsunami
- Runaway

Some would argue that in an ideal world all entrepreneurs would follow a structure. But SUSS is all about realism.

The SUSS pathway allows entrepreneurs to jump into the process at different stages. By doing this, 6 important successes are achieved.

- Understanding the way your Mind Set affects your likelihood of success
- Reduces your workload
- Encourages you to check if you have found a real Pain Point
- Creates at least one safety net to prevent high cost failure – money, time and emotion
- Encourages a Fast Fail for bad ideas with minimum cost
- Provides a clear pathway for you to replay the SUSS Sequence if your first idea does not work

In this Chapter you will specifically learn

1. To Understand the Start Up Safe Sequence and how it compares to traditional approaches
2. How the SUSS encourages you to think like you would on a game of Snakes and Ladders
3. To consider your own starting position in the Sequence
4. To know when to dump an idea
5. To think like a Professional Entrepreneur by learning that an idea that is not strong enough to invest in, should be dumped early. Very early in the process.
6. To fully understand the time, money and emotional costs of forcing bad ideas to market

There is also an exercise task work for you to do yourself.

4.2. Understand Start Up Safe Sequence compare it to traditional approaches

Classic Approach

The classic approach to investigating and launching a new business is shown below.

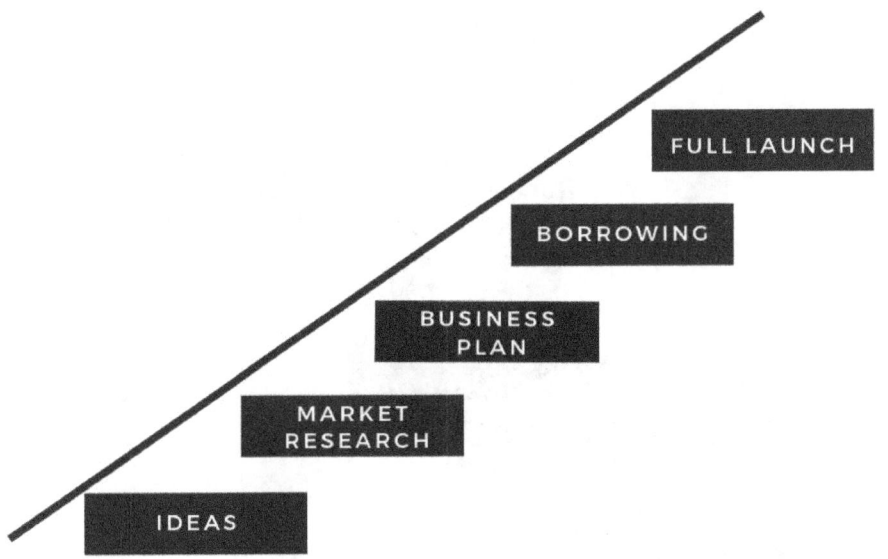

Let's run through this briefly.

Most conventional start up and business training offered to first time entrepreneurs is based on borrowing to get the business started.

Business plans in the classical approach are based on getting loans from classical banks.

This is a model that is obsolete and for a time before the 2008 crash. It existed for banks as the main source of loans and even pre- internet in terms of product testing and market research techniques.

Banks are not lending so easily to start ups and crowdfunding is on the rise of course. The days of putting on a suit to borrow money from the bank prior to a full launch are gone. Even banks will say the same; their focus has shifted far more towards educating start ups, which is to their credit.

Market research tools are significantly improved, but more people recognise market research is not reliable or safe for testing actual **buying intent** of customers.

Business planning has moved from the 30 page epic to more compact single page processes.

Most importantly ideas can be more easily and inexpensively tested in the market, before borrowing due to digital imaging mock ups, explainer videos, CAD and 3D prototype printing.

So bring in a better way the Start Up Safe Sequence or SSUS for short.

The Start Up Safe Sequence or SSUS

Now let us take a look at the SUSS and make some comparisons between Mind Sets.

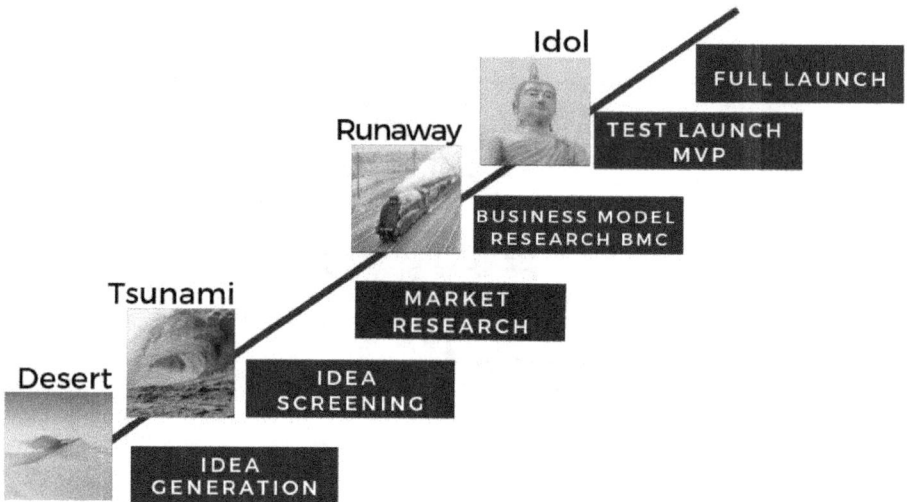

At a glance one can see several major differences between the Classic and SUSS methods. There are 6 stages in SUSS rather than 5.

More than One Starting Point

You will see that the 4 Mind Sets come in at different stages in the sequence. Why? Because that is real life! No matter how much I or any other voice suggests all entrepreneurs start with idea generation, it is not going to happen. We will examine this in more detail later.

No Borrowing and Low Cost Launches

The Classic Borrowing stage is not on the SUSS model at all.

The reason the Classic Borrowing stage is not on SUSS is because a successful test launch can and is often delivered for minimal investment (possibly a few hundred up to two thousand pounds maximum). This is normally within the reach of the entrepreneur and does not bite into savings or redundancy pay from the last job. Not all businesses can start without borrowing - of course not. But every business CAN start off with a Test Launch. If a Test Launch goes well it can create cash flow to reduce (or even remove the need for borrowing). It can certainly improve the chances of gaining funding if you can demonstrate real sales when you ask for money. This is especially important for those many entrepreneurs unable to borrow for credit reasons and for my beloved Bouncepreneurs who have lost a previous business and have to bounce back in business often on a shoe-string.

SUSS Business Model and SUSS Test Launch

Sorry about the jargon folks! - There are two new items (which will really help you). Firstly, the Business Plan stage is replaced by the SUSS Business Plan. And the SUSS Test Launch. Both use the Pain Point as a guiding principle. I will explain both in detail. Do not worry. For now here is a quick description.

The SUSS Business Model has nine segments which form the building blocks for the business model in a nice one-page format. It allows entrepreneurs to build a strong business model, because you can focus on it segment by segment. It also prompts careful research to establish what you do not know.

SUSS Test Launch is a development of the popular Minimum Viable Product (MVP) method. It is a product or service OR simulation of the product or service built at a very low cost in time and money. It is just enough to be able to demonstrate what you have AND capture real sales with early adopters. It is a great way to test your idea to see if customers will **actually** buy it. Uber and Apple both started with this approach. But there are many more - so did Facebook, Twitter, iPhone. But it is not just in software, manufacturers and retailers like BDRThermea and Zappos, made it work too. It worked for them and it can work for you.

Ideas – Generation and Screening

You can now see that the Ideas stage is in two completely different stages of the SUSS Idea Generation and Idea Screening. This is done to avoid a problem so common in start ups – judging ideas too early!

Mixing the Streams Problem between Idea Generation and Idea Screening

Some readers may recall in the Ghostbusters Movies the heroes had special guns which fired Proton Streams and disaster would follow if the streams of two guns crossed. So remember you must never "Cross the Streams" between Idea Generation and Idea Screening.

START UP SAFE SEQUENCE
SUSS DESERT

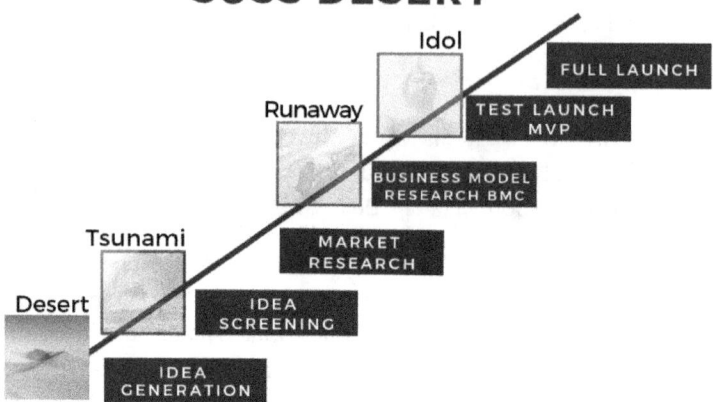

4.3. Desert Mind Set Start Point

If you are of the Desert Mind Set I recommend your SUSS start point to be IDEA GENERATION.

You struggle to find ideas remember. But this is a blessing in disguise. Why? Because you are giving yourself the opportunity to follow the full SUSS Sequence without compromise. As a Desert Mind Set I recommend you start by picking from the WIDEST range of good ideas using the SUSS Idea Generation method, which is explained in full later.

What Desert Minds Need to Work On

The Desert Mind Set as we know finds it very difficult to identify any ideas. So without the Idea Generation stage they are not even going to get onto the Sequence at all. There is no point planning business models, launches and so on if you cannot choose an idea. So the genuine Desert Mind Set should pay special attention to starting at the Idea Generation teaching coming up later in the book.

The Khabarov Desert Mind Set

In the Gulag escape film "The Way Back," actor Mark Strong is superb as prisoner Khabarov, reminding me of several "entrepreneurs" I mistook for having Desert Mind Sets.

They are Khabarovs. In the movie Khabarov secretly tells Janusz (a new arrival) he plans to escape. But in order to maintain his own spirits Khabarov repeatedly and selfishly latches on to newcomers to discuss escape plans, but never follows through. If you can see a little of yourself in Khabarov, that is you come up with ideas and dismiss them immediately, telling others you have no ideas, then I say hold your nerve. Go through Idea Generation and Screening fully. Some Khabarovs are darker characters. They are energy vampires enthralled by, but terrified of entrepreneurship. They will never act and Khabarovs are to be avoided!

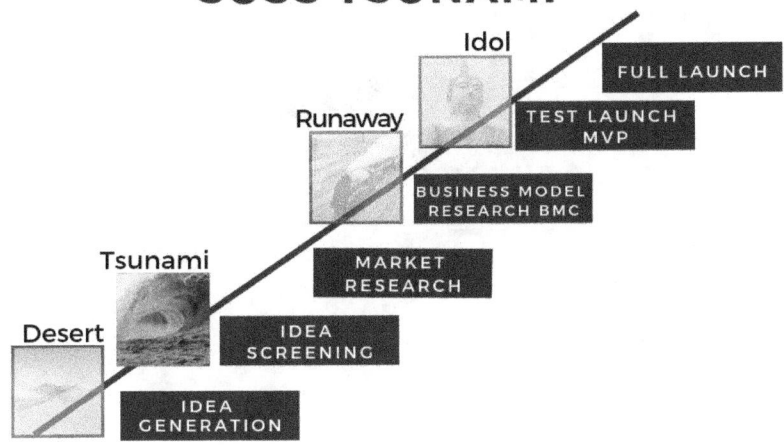

4.4. Tsunami Mind Start Point

If you are a Tsunami Mind Set, your problem is not generating ideas. It is Screening them down to your best options, and then being able to commit to taking <u>one</u> idea forward into Market Research.

What Tsunamis Need to Work On

Firstly, just because you have lots of ideas, it does not mean they are necessarily good ideas. This is especially true if all your ideas all originate from a single flawed assumption. But generally Tsunamis have enough ideas of quality to find one to move forward with. The two main challenges the Tsunamis amongst you face are:-

1. Which of my ideas is the best one?
2. How do I switch off the idea flow when I am progressing a chosen idea?

Your start point in the SUSS is Idea Screening. You will learn how to pick you best ideas. Rest assured you will have that well covered. It is a very learnable skill to learn and nothing to fear.

But the second challenge, switching off the ideas flow, well that is a tougher challenge entirely, if you are of the Tsunami Mind Set.

Tsunamis have a habit of self-sabotage. That's right, you will advance an idea to launch, but then if something else catches their focus you will lose interest in the idea you are developing, in favour of your new one. Worse, still you may do it repeatedly. It can be a Fear of Failure driving this Mind Set.

But if the Tsunami can turn their huge creative energy into sticking with a good idea and being creative in the detail such as branding, selling and customer service delight, then success commonly follows.

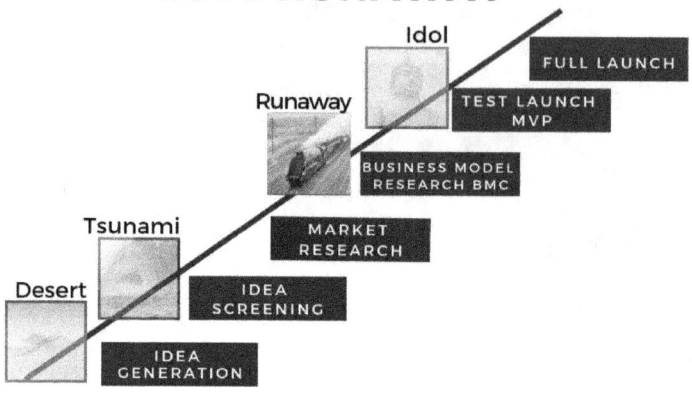

4.5. Runaway Mind Start Point

The Runaway Mind Set makes entrepreneurs into express trains that are out of control and surging down the track at top speed. Chances of a crash are high!

As you are a Runaway there is little point in telling you to be different, you will not listen. You won't! So the best I can do is to encourage you to be diligent at the Business Model stage of SUSS.

What Runaways Need to Work On

The Runaway Mind Set is often driven by financial pressure and is too receptive to business ideas offered by other people.

But it does not matter how slick and polished the marketing materials that a multi-level marketing or franchise outfit offers you, the market potential ALWAYS needs to be checked. This is also true if a friend, relative or colleague is pitching you the idea. You still need market research.

Furthermore, a poor idea can still be exposed at the Business Model and Test Launch phases of the SUSS. If you are looking at a Multi-Level Marketing (MLM) or franchise go out with others already doing it, without the franchise sales manager being present. Hear from others if it works.

If you do see yourself in the Runaway Mind Set category, try to remain cool and calm no matter what pressure you are under to generate money.

- Check out the claims of any "pre-packaged" businesses you are offered
- Do work on the SUSS Business Plan Stage (to follow)
- Never, fully launch (full investment in a franchise for example) without a test launch.

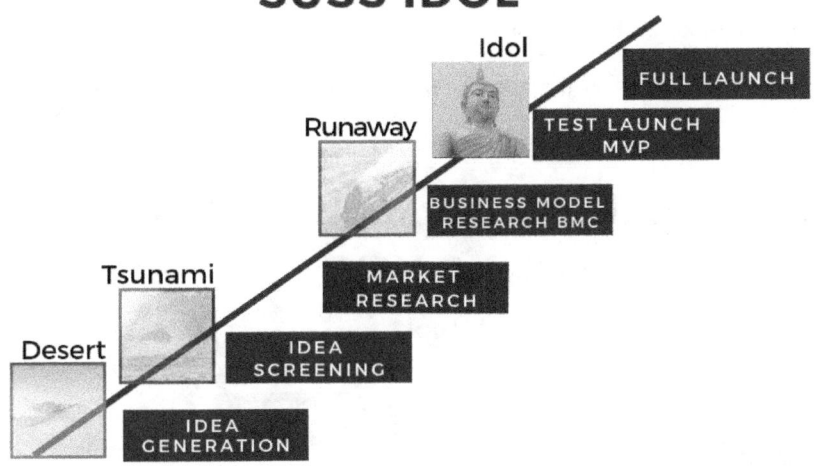

4.6. Idol Mind Set Start Point

The normal start point for the Idol Mind Set is Full Launch. As Idol's are the most stubborn of all the Mind Sets the SUSS entry point we recommend for you is to start with a Test Launch. At the very least you will conserve your money if your beloved idea does not sell.

What Idols Need to Work On

Unlike the other 3 Mind Sets I cannot easily tell the Idol Mind Set what to work on. You are backing yourself and believe in your idea. Who am I to "rain on your parade?"

But as someone who has worked with over 300 entrepreneurs whose ventures have failed, I can tell you it is not pretty. So if you will not listen to me for yourself, listen for the sake of your family, because they will be the ones who feel the real pain if you fail. They will go with out, they may see the family car towed away.

All I am asking of you, is that even if you do not do everything in the SUSS. Just do the Test Launch. Go for it with all your energy, skills and belief. I wish you tremendous success. If you do it as a Test Launch you do not lose all your money, you can still ramp up if it works OR pivot your idea slightly and retry the Test Launch if it does not quite work first time.

Nothing you do on the Test Launch will be wasted. Nothing! You can use it all if you ramp up to full launch. But may just safeguard spending your savings and 12 months of your life!

4.7 How the Professional Entrepreneur Fox Mind Set Does it?

Many of you may be asking, I see where Idol, Runaway, Desert and Tsunami Mind Sets start, but not Fox. The Fox Mind Set does not always start at the same point. Sometimes Foxes start at Idea Generation or Idea Screening. Occasionally they will start at Market Research stage, if a notable idea is presented to them or they have a Eureka moment!

But the Fox Mind Set never ever starts higher than the Market Research Stage. You can see this in the Chart below.

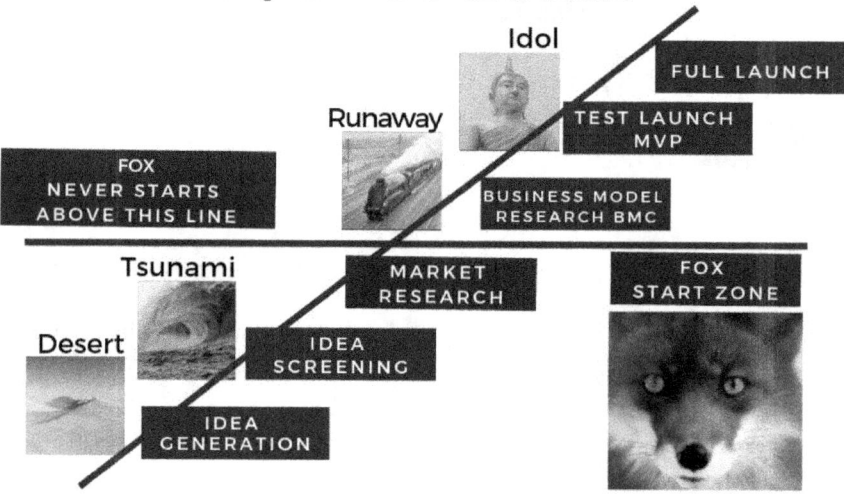

Why does the Fox Mind Set never start above the line? Simple. Risk. Foxes never assume they know what the customer sees as a Pain Point. They always test. Also, the amount of work you have to do increases with every stage along the line. So it saves time and money to drop poor ideas early.

Why the Fox Mind Entrepreneurs Start at the Beginning of the Sequence	
Sequence Stage	Minimum Time Needed
Idea Generation	1 day
Idea Screening	2 days
Market Research	7 days
Business Model Research	10 – 14 days
Test Launch	90 days * including planning
Launch	180 days

Foxes think, why would you launch an idea at an advanced stage, when win, lose or draw you will spend 6 months to a year figuring out whether the business is viable?

Fox Mind Sets would rather realise the idea is not viable at screening or market research stages and save lots of time and money.

4.8. It's Not All Ladders Going One Way

Too many entrepreneurs think the investigation of their business ideas is a one way street, just ladders heading towards their launch. But the best entrepreneurs are not emotionally attached to their business ideas and they see the process more like a game of Snakes and Ladders.

Ladders will take you up and Snakes will take you down! But the Snakes are as friendly to you as the Ladders. You have to understand that.

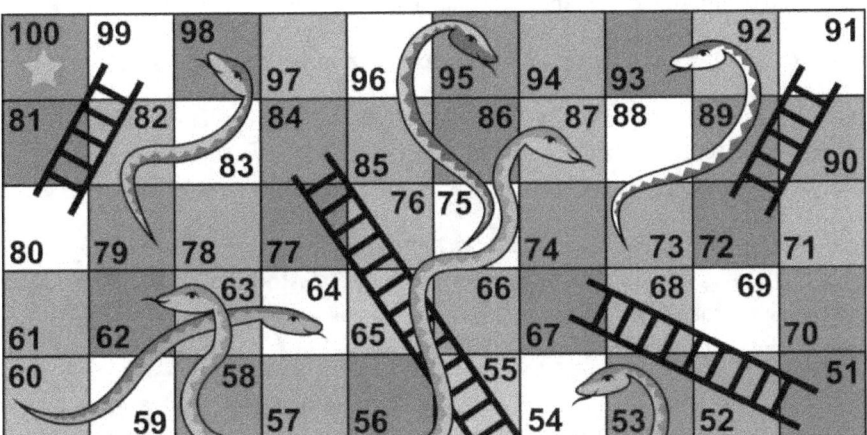

When you play Snakes and Ladders and hit a snake, you go downwards, but not backwards, as soon you are moving forward again and may well win.

In generating business ideas, hitting a snake simply means the idea is flawed and needs considerable rework OR to be abandoned altogether. This means you have to go back down the sequence to start looking at a new idea.

Remember there is at least a year of your life on the line here and maybe your savings.

4.9. What you have learned in this Chapter

You have learned that no matter what your Mind Set is, you can reduce risk by building in some safety checks. You have also seen how the best Entrepreneurs (Fox Mind Set) start at different points in the SUSS, but never launch without Market Research.

The Snakes and Ladders example has shown you that Choosing an Idea wisely demands you sometimes have to go down the snake and well as up the ladder to be successful.

Now in the following Chapters I will show you how to implement each of the SUSS stages. In the next Chapter we take a really good look at SUSS Idea Generation.

5. SUSS Idea Generation

5.1. What You Are Going to Learn in This Chapter

In this Chapter you will be shown some proven techniques to help you Choose an Idea. You will be generating 10-20 ideas for your Safer Start Up. You will be shown two variations on brainstorming plus Online methods to produce ideas.

If you already have an idea or ideas, this is not a problem but an asset. I refer to them as "Introduced Ideas." Your introduced idea or ideas are simply ideas you already have before you start the Idea Generation stage. For Idols and Runaways you will have a single idea. Tsunamis you will have lots I am sure and Desert Mind Sets start from fresh, struggling for a little inspiration. But very importantly even Introduced Ideas can be improved with these techniques.

They are just added into the 10 -20 other ideas WITHOUT special treatment or preference.

Brainstorming is a great way to generate AND improve start up ideas. Many readers will have been involved in brainstorming previously, so it is not an alien concept. Essentially people sit together with the idea of coming up with some new ideas.

You know in my last book I gave entrepreneurs about ten methods of brainstorming to choose from. But I have learnt that many entrepreneurs have real anxiety about brainstorming. So I have decided to provide a much simpler approach for readers. In fact I am only going to offer you two methods. Yes just two and you will quickly know which one is right for you.

For those of you who have brainstormed before, both these methods may be a little different, so keep an open mind. But your past experience will be useful especially when it comes to letting ideas flow without criticism. The two methods are:-

   a. Brainwriting 365
   b. Business Model Brainstorming BMB

I have stated that different Mind Sets will enter the SUSS at different points. I cannot stop you doing this of course. But I STRONGLY recommend, hope and even pray to convince some of you Idols and Runaways to use the whole sequence.

Before we move on, here are two quick reminders for you.

Paint Points are more than ideas, when you find a Pain Point you find a strong opportunity.

Remember the Ghostbusters. You must never "Cross the Streams" between Idea Generation and Idea Streaming. This Chapter is where you come up with ideas NOT where you scrutinise them.

In this Chapter you will learn where you can draw your 10 - 20 ideas from:-

- Life Experience Idea Generation
- Your introduced Idol or Runaway Idea
- Classic Brainstorming Idea Generation methods
- Online Idea Generation methods

5.2. Using Life Experiences for Idea Generation

Many of the most successful businesses in history have come from ideas for products and services that individuals have witnessed first-hand in their:-

- Personal life
- Family life
- Work both current and past jobs
- Social occasions

Here are a couple of great examples of business ideas that came from life experiences.

Example: GoPro cameras - Nick Woodman was surfing in Bali. The selfie craze was taking off around the World. Nick wanted great selfies of himself in the surf. He fixed a 35mm camera to his hand with an elastic band, but it was not a great solution. Nick became inspired to create a waterproof camera with a wrist harness. His design, now famous as GoPro, created a market now worth $6.9 billion.

Example: Black and Decker Workmate - Colin Hickman's inspiration for the Workmate came as he was building a wardrobe at home. When he cut the leg off an expensive Swedish chair he was using as a sawhorse and his wife saw red! So Colin invented a simple, multifunctional bench combining both sawhorse and vice on a foldable alloy frame.

I am encouraging you to think about ideas (PAIN POINTS) that come from your own personal experiences. They can also come from experiences you witness, or are told about by your partner, children, friends, colleagues and strangers.

What I would encourage you to do is to take each of the idea threads shown in the graphic below and think about it on its own for a while. Ideally a whole day!

Let's take your health experiences for an example. You might be in hospital or your elderly parent is receiving treatment. Just get this situation into your mind. Think about the PAIN POINTS you had or saw.

I strongly recommend keeping a note pad, or phone app with you to write down your ideas with you 24/7 365. Eureka moments can wake you up at any time of the night or come to life on the bus or at any other time during your day.

Finally, you might want to try doing this through meditation. Now I am no expert in meditation and will not try to be. But by quietly meditating on one of the Idea Threads you will be able to bring solid ideas into your brain. It works.

Give it a try!

LIFE EXPERIENCE IDEA GENERATION

PAY ATTENTION

Pay attention to these areas.

Think about Pain Points you, your family or others have experienced.

IDEA THREADS
- Your Health Experiences
- Hobbies
- Family
- Your Areas of Expertise
- Job and Past Jobs
- Past Training
- Education
- Friends
- Chance Idea Finds
- Social Activity

TO THESE AREAS

Think about Pain Points from your professional and educational experiences.

© Bouncepreneurs.com

5.3. Top Tips for Effective Idea Generation

Before we get into the methods, do remember

You Need More Than One Idea - Remember your top idea may fail at three further stages

- Screening
- Market Research
- Test Launch

So it really is important that you develop several ideas at this Brainstorming stage.

Some tips for you to consider.

- Getting People Involved – Most entrepreneurs are really quite nervous about asking people to get involved. I have seen entrepreneurs (who would look at home in a MMA fight) almost shaking at the thought of asking someone to get involved. Funnily I often see others reluctant to do brainstorming because of fear of leaking some TOP SECRET business idea to competitors.
- Listen! How can you hope to sell to customers if you will not make contact with individuals at your business testing stage?
- Do not fear; let me put you at ease. You can run these sessions in your home. I would try to avoid friends and family if you can help it, or at least keep their numbers down.
- A good way of relaxing everybody is to make a nice meal for everybody afterwards. Big bowl of spaghetti and a glass of red, for example. Plus it is a nice way to thank people for their time.
- If you are planning the Business Model Brainstorming approach, don't be frightened to ask individuals in your industry already, people are incredibly generous with ideas. Get a couple of people in digital marketing to be involved, they will often open up the product list very wide.

- I would consider a teenager or two. It is surprising in my experience the impact the can have on your session.
- Remember there are no bad ideas in brainstorming. **Never** critique other people's ideas no matter how zany or crazy they might sound.
- Remember - it won't be your only business. You will have others. You are building an Empire. So if you have a second or third great idea, then save it, as you may be returning to it – even in 10 years' time.
- You may come up with ideas that you don't like very much, but keep them in the process. Remember "where's there's muck there is brass." There is money in work no-one else wants to do.
- Brainstorming does not have to be your only source of ideas. Start a notes page on your phone or a little paper black book. Keep your eyes and ears open for problems that annoy consumers or businesses. Throw them all into the pot along with your brainstorming ideas.

5.4. Brainwriting 635

This variation on Brainstorming is especially good if you have Desert or Tsunami Mind Set.

desert

This process generates LOTS of ideas. I mean lots. This is the main problem for you if you are in the Idea Desert right? Plus it is super easy to manage and you do not need a specialist administrator or moderator to run it.

tsunami

Those who have many ideas will also benefit from the Brainwriting 635 method, because it provides a great channelling tool for their energy and creativity. It also provides a place to really go for it with the ideas. I recommend the entrepreneur is actually one of the idea generators rather than the moderator.

Like traditional brainstorming, Brainwriting 635 involves a group of people sitting together to come up with ideas. But 635 is far less chaotic, more structured and easier to manage.

It is much easier to manage that brainstorming and provides the following benefits:-

- The method does not need a trained moderator, you can moderate yourself

- If the participants see a notably strong idea they will take it further.
- Every member of the group is involved evenly (this is very challenging to achieve in general brainstorming).
- There is no premature discussion by the participants, which ensures each person can contribute without doubts about their ideas arising from earlier conversations.
- You can populate your group with experts and people who will have different viewpoints from each other
- Later on the creator of a particularly strong idea can be identified, which provides motivation to the group

How does it Work?

In a nutshell

- **6** people
- Write down **3** Ideas (ideally on a simple form – see below)
- In **5** minutes
- That is where the name 635 comes from

Now once the 6 people have written down 3 ideas in 5 minutes that is a round. What happens next is the form is passed to their neighbour on the right. Then you repeat the 635 process again as Round 2. Then this goes on to Round 3 right until Round 5.

How to Start – Start by presenting the challenge, which is finding a new business idea for you the entrepreneur.

You can start with a 5 minute introduction about yourself, describing:-

- Current situation
- Work experience – go right back and cover it all, but be brief and punchy
- Skills and education
- Your family situation and home
- Any assets you have – e.g. a vintage car, horses, access to your local church hall and kitchen
- Languages and knowledge of other cultures
- Your hobbies
- Your personality
- Things you do and don't enjoy doing

Keep this presentation to an ABSOLUTE maximum of 5 minutes – otherwise your people will get bored and far less creative with their ideas. **Do not send this out in advance of the session** in writing, present it just before you start. That will ruin the session. Ideally use a flip chart, or show some pictures, but no "death by PowerPoint."

Now you can set out the Challenge for your group.

I need ideas for a new business for myself. What do you think could work for me?

Tell the Group they can be as wacky as they wish. They can have ideas that are linked to your experience and past. OR they can write down ideas that do not directly relate to you.

It is better to give out a form, like the one shown below. Make it a full A4 size; write the name of the person in the left hand column.

Do ask participants to write clearly, also not to be too complex in their descriptions. Sometimes with the 635 approach some participants do not explain themselves clearly. So suggest they are brief and concise.

The form is well worth it and prevents any ideas being lost in the chaos of normal brainstorming. When people see what has been written by other members of the group, it stimulates fresh thinking from them.

Be clear that the participants must pass the sheet to the person on their right and this prevents any confusion. Control this and do not let it deviate.

BRAINWRITING 6 3 5			
Person	Idea 1	Idea 2	Idea 3
Joe			
Sammy			
Adrian			
Erica			
Wioletta			
Amanda			

So once you have finished the group will have produced a LOT of ideas. In each of the 5 minute rounds, each of the 6 participants has produced 3 ideas.

That is 108 ideas!

Now that will take you out of the Idea Desert. If you are of the Tsunami Mind Set, you will find it very interesting to see if others see the same opportunities as you do.

5.5. Business Model Brainstorming (BMB)

Business Model brainstorming is very different from 635 Brainwriting and especially suits the Runaway and Idol mind sets.

runaway

idol

The truth is that no matter how hard one tries, many people are extremely closely tied to their original idea. No amount of persuasion will change their minds. Later, in the SUSS, the Test Launch safety net soon shows if it is a dud idea. So I selected a brainstorming method that is sympathetic to entrepreneurs with a great desire to launch a specific idea.

For both Runaway and Idol Mind sets the BMB model expands your original idea. It is also very good for shifting entrepreneurs away from thinking about their business as a Job they work **in** to a Business they work **on**. Why? Because it naturally migrates to scalable ventures!

This BMB method is simple to use, but requires care selecting members of your brainstorming group.

This is not a well-known method like 635 Brainwriting. In fact it is a bit of a hybrid.

I suggest it as a great method for Idol and Runaway Mind Sets. Why?

- It does not "pour cold water" over ideas you may be very passionate about
- It respects your intellect and experience
- It creates an acceptable level of challenge
- It creates several options around your core idea you might not have previously thought of
- It meshes very well with the next short-listing phase

As the name suggests it is brainstorming to improve business models and especially expands the scope of the entrepreneur's thinking on how the core of the idea could be delivered.

This method has two very strong advantages, which are:-

- It allows the brainstorming group to be packed with people with in depth knowledge of the business concept and for it THEN to be significantly advanced WITHOUT being seen to critique the logic of the Idols entrepreneur's original idea.
- Secondly, in the case of the Runaway Mind Set it gently reverses then" train" back to a more critical test and idea expansion process, before the entrepreneur crashes into a poorly prepared launch.

How Does It Work

You need 4-8 people, with 6 being the ideal number.

You will need a flip chart and pens

Two of your participants should be experts in something outside of your specialisation – for example in digital marketing or authoring. The remainder should know your industry, market and customers pretty well.

It is better if the entrepreneur themselves is NEITHER a participant NOR a moderator. Given the traits of this mind set you will try and "bend" the group. Believe me you will! I have been in sessions where the entrepreneur's body language alone affected the group and she didn't even say anything. Rolling eyes, shaking head, huffing and puffing all influence the group badly.

So if you are sitting in on the group please be a silent still observer and NOTHING else. Ideally out of the eye line of your participants.

If circumstances mean you have to be the moderator, stay neutral, record and do not chide or influence the other members at all!

Start with a Simple Statement. Only show this at the beginning of the session, not beforehand. When you are inviting participants, do not show the detail. Just tell them it is a brainstorming session to help you in your entrepreneurial journey.

Also give the participants the following statement printed out on a piece of paper at the beginning of the session. Allow one minute for participants to digest it then start.

Have flip board and pen ready, participants need to see everything you have written down.

Instructions to Participants

Your host (NAME) is planning to start a new business. They will shortly give you a 30 second explanation of the business they are planning.

It is your role to generate as many alternative ideas as possible which are linked to your host's preferred industry; they should not be the same business idea as they have presented, but variations or extensions of it are welcome.

Please do not ask your host for further clarification. Just begin throwing out ideas

You host should not engage in dialogue with you after their 30 second explanation has been given.

You should not critique the ideas generated at all

You can build on ideas of your fellow participants. Generate as many ideas as possible

The process should last no more than 30 minutes.

Many thanks. Now let's start, right now, without delay

Your statement should relate to the general area of trade you are planning to go into. For example:

"I am going to be a personal trainer in the Fitness Industry".

Original Idea	Extensions of the Original Idea	
PERSONAL TRAINER IN FITNESS INDUSTRY	Make protein bars	Write an eBook
	Sell fitness equipment	Produce a video workout series
	Make a fitness machine	Do local marketing for the fitness industry
	Multi-level marketing of fitness supplements	Sell fitness clothing
	Write a fitness blog	Workout App

So in the example above we see our Start Up entrepreneur planning to be a personal trainer in the fitness industry. But the Business Model Brainstorming throws out lots of alternatives. A good goal is to generate 20 + alternatives.

5.6. Online Idea Generation

I do not have to tell anyone about power of the internet for finding things and ideas is no different.

The number one tip is to remember you are looking for lots of ideas at this stage, not just one. We all gravitate towards a favourite but keep going. I would suggest at least 10 and ideally 20 ideas is a good number.

<u>Keyword phrases in general</u>

Social media tools and search engines all have a search bar. Type a phrase that it has seen before and recorded (indexed), it displays results that match or come near your phrase. Most often you will get a count on the number of hits or articles associated with the phrase or keyword. You will use this further in Idea Screening, but in this stage just get those ideas flowing. It simply provides a general idea of interest levels.

<u>Google</u>

Firstly if you simply search for "Business Ideas," or "Start Up Ideas" you will get masses of returns. From a basic search you will mainly get online business ideas – and lots of them. You could easily get a list of 100 in 15 minutes. Here. Are a couple of search examples?

- 27 "Easy to Start" Online Business Ideas
- 7 Online Business Ideas That Could Make You Rich

But Google can tell you a lot more. It can tell you what people are looking at. What they are looking at, complaining about and commenting on are sometimes Paint Points and they make the best ideas.

Google AdWords offers a free keyword tool so it is easy to find which keywords are generating the most searches per month. Within Google AdWords you find the Google Keyword Planner. If you use this free tool you can see which products and services people are spending on advertising. This really does help generate your own ideas for creating something new. In the Market Research Chapter we will look at Google Trends, which illuminates the performance of your chosen keywords over time, giving you real insight into trends.

Pinterest

It is a very powerful source of ideas for creative businesses in my view

- You can lift a successful idea from one part of the world to your own.
- It is also good for seeing the prime motivations and activities of specific groups.
- Great for spotting aspiration through the boards of influencers
- You can see if and what ideas pinners are linking to ecommerce and other selling systems

Because Pinterest uses hashtags on pins, you can search as broadly or narrowly as you like and find popular niche pins that may show or spark a great idea.

What makes Pinterest really special is that users can monitor comments without other users seeing the views. You can gauge how people think of individual pins and this can really help on ideas.

In my opinion Pinterest's comments section gives a more user-friendly and inspiring way of spotting new ideas than other social media sites.

Facebook and LinkedIn for Idea Generation

When using Facebook or LinkedIn for idea generation, entrepreneurs tend to start with a line of enquiry linked to a favoured idea already. So they look for groups linked to the idea. This restricts the scope of ideas we are seeking.

The idea-specific groups of course are a treasure trove of comments on that industry, product or service and highly useful but best left until Idea Screening.

Business Competition Shows on TV or YouTube

Business Competition Shows like Dragon's Den are great. But there are other business TV shows that are more about securing investment and turnarounds which are just as useful for finding ideas.

If you can get hold of a whole series/season online you can pick up so many ideas. This works in three ways:-

- The entrepreneurs have good ideas which you can do too
- The judges critiques allow you to see what better ideas are made of
- All these shows have large second screen audiences (commenting on each episode) you can hear what others think of ideas and critically whether they believe the idea fixes a specific problem or not.

Everybody seems to go for Dragons Den or Shark Tank; it is made in 30 countries by the way, so there are a lot of episodes to cull ideas from. I would highly recommend Marcus Lemonis in The Profit (personally I think it is the best one). Others in hospitality are Jon Taffer in Bar Rescue and the stellar bright and experienced Alex Polizzi in the Hotel Inspector and The Fixer.

Twitter

Big companies and government work Twitter hard. They welcome customer feedback and it is in the public domain in full view on Twitter. So this allows you to go in and look at questions being asked by customers – both consumers and B2B. This allows you to spot Pain Points and gaps you may be able to fill. Their comments and complaints will often help you shape ideas on what customers really do want and what they perceive to be problems with current suppliers products or service.

Flipboard

Flipboard is a great tool for Idea Generation. It will provide details of topics aligned to your Idea Generation Spectrum. Plus it plays a later role in the SUSS in Idea Screening too. It offers a huge number of currently trending topics, but the categorisation makes it easy to use for ideas.

5.7. What you have learned in this Chapter

In this Chapter you have focused on Idea Generation, aware of the need to generate 10 -20 ideas without putting them under any type of scrutiny or screening.

You have also been shown how to bring the process closer to you as an individual by using your Life Experience Idea Generation

You have learnt some online and some offline ways of generating ideas.

Well done on generating your Ideas. Now on to Idea Screening.

6. SUSS Idea Screening

6.1. What You Are Going to Learn in This Chapter

You are now at the Idea Screening stage of the Start Up Safe Sequence (SUSS).

So now you have 10 to 20 ideas.

Congratulations for your self-control in not "Crossing the Streams." You've restrained yourself and focused on generating ideas. This will really pay off.

The goal of this Chapter is to identify your top three ideas. You will take the best one of the ideas forward to the next stage of the SUSS – Market Research.

You need to hold two ideas in reserve, because your top idea can still fail at later stage in the SUSS and you may need to come back for idea number two or even three.

In this Chapter you will take <u>each</u> of your 10 - 20 ideas and run them through 16 screening questions. We call this the CAKE process Clarity, Alignment, Kooky, Evolution – 4 groups of 4 questions.

6.2. The Process Explained

The 4 Idea Screening Filters used in the SUSS have been chosen after a significant amount of research into how entrepreneurs effectively screen ideas. Again we are sympathetic to the real Mind Sets of Entrepreneurs and even make a concession to the Runaways and Idols amongst you. You can see the overview on the next page. There is a nice form at the end of this Chapter to help you.

Do remember, you are following a sequence. In an ideal world you would have all the information on all your ideas from the next 3 stages in the process at your disposal now. But you don't have:-

- Market Research
- Business Modelling
- Test Launch

The task of testing 10 - 20 ideas through this stage is simply too much work. So at this stage you will have to make informed decisions with the information available to you.

Some of the screening questions are especially important and are called Killer Questions. If your idea fails on any one of these questions, OR you simply do not know the answer, do not move this idea forward. Remember, it is simply not safe and we are all about reduction of risk!

<u>Coming up in this Chapter</u>

a) Overview of 4 CAKE Screening
b) Detailed explanation of each of the questions
c) A single page version of the CAKE Screening Questionnaire, followed by two examples
d) Finally, a task to assess all your ideas and compare them, allowing you to select your top 3 ideas to go forward into the Market Research stage of the SUSS.

IDEA SCREENING
4 FILTERS
Safer Start Up Sequence

Clarity

Evolution

Alignment
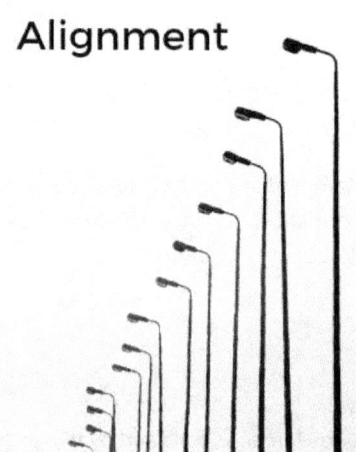

Kooky

Bouncepreneurs.com

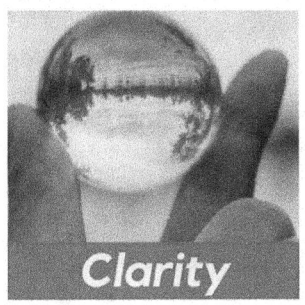

SSUP IDEA SCREENING

6.3. Clarity is the first slice of the CAKE Idea Screening process. You will need to put all your ideas through these 4 questions. If **any** of your ideas fail to get a positive answer on the Killer questions, you should set it aside, drop it and move forward with your remaining ideas.

Is it really a Painkiller or just a Vitamin? (Killer Question)

Now is the time to really decide on this. Do you really, really see this as a Painkiller solution for customers? You will find out for sure in market research and test launch. But is this idea absolutely going to ease pain. Or is it a really just a Vitamin? Answer honestly, to the best of your ability.

Avatar – do you see your customer type?

Are you seeing a customer type (or Avatar) fairly clearly in your own mind? Do you see their age, sex, interests and location? If it is B2B do you clearly see the industry or the industry customers will be in? How many? The way they make decisions? No-one sees their Avatar perfectly at this stage and it can change. In the Netherlands electric bike suppliers thought elderly people would be the biggest market. But it was kids going to school. The electric bike allowed them to travel in inclement weather, reducing the parent's need to drive them.

Will it generate revenue within 90 days in your bank? (Killer Question)

This is a Yes or No question. Are you absolutely certain you will have money IN your bank account within 90 days from launch? 90 days is the absolute maximum by the way. With my clients I normally make it 30 days and sometimes 60. If you have development work to do which will prevent you actually selling, drop this idea. If you are relying on tender work, forget this idea – you cannot control you income timelines. Finally if your business is seasonal (nothing wrong with that) and you are launching in the wrong season, think again, or wait until the season is right to test launch.

Is it financially feasible to test launch?

Can you afford to test launch this idea? Think hard, you really can test launch on very little money. If you need costly items to test launch, then think again. Really rethink. There is always a way to launch on the cheap. If you are pitching to investors and planning to use the test launch to demonstrate the business case to invest, then you still need to test on the cheap! If the idea is complex and needs lots of capital you do not have, then drop it.

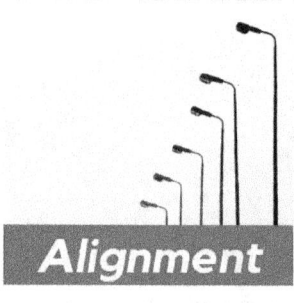

SSUP IDEA SCREENING

6.4. Alignment is the second slice of questions you need to run each of your ideas against. You should have lost a few ideas in the Clarity phase of the questions. The Alignment phase looks more at how you are personally positioned against each of your ideas. Some of your ideas you will feel closely aligned to. Others you won't have such a match. Try the questions on each of your ideas.

How much knowledge do you have?

Do you know much about this idea? How much knowledge do you have about the specific product or service? Ask yourself honestly. Are you a "Novice" or an "Old Hand" in this market? Most importantly, is the gap between the knowledge you have now and the knowledge you need to make this idea a success, bridgeable by hard study and learning? Ask – "Do I have enough knowledge?"

Is this an idea that is close to your interests?

Does this idea come out of a specific interest or hobby you have? Perhaps you have been an avid historian all your life and your new business is in battlefield tours. Maybe it is connected to an innovation that you were not allowed to pursue at work, but always interested you. Perhaps you have always loved to cook and this idea extends from your hobby.

Most importantly ask yourself – "Do I have a real affiliation with this idea?"

Do you have a talent linked to this idea?

Talent can mean a number of things, not just being able to entertain people or be great at a sport. You may be a brilliant company accountant and want to educate small businesses. Perhaps you are a genius at lawn care and were head-hunted by Wimbledon. Maybe you can build CRM systems in a fraction of the time needed by most large teams. Ask – "Do I have a talent linked to this idea?"

Do you have enough experience around this idea?

Launching a business is hard enough on its own, without trying to learn new skills at the same time. Years ago I planned to launch a wooden furniture business. But the truth is I knew nothing about professional wood-working. In fact give me a saw and I would soon be fingerless! If your idea is in a high growth area, where few have experience, then it may be worthwhile. But generally ask yourself – "Do I have enough experience of this idea to make it work?"

SSUP IDEA SCREENING

6.5. Kooky is the third slice of the CAKE Idea Screening stage. The definition of Kooky is according to Dictionary.com *"of, like, or pertaining to a kook; eccentric, strange, or foolish."*

In this slice of questions we make room for ideas and concepts that you probably will not see in classic text books, but they are worth looking at anyway. I apologise is advance for contradicting myself against other parts of this book. But too many brilliant Start Ups were laughed at so I have to allow some radical thinking against which to test your ideas.

Is your idea simple enough?

For the Idols and Runaways out there, well done for trying Idea Screening. We know you are "joined at the hip," to your main idea, so please check it against these questions. Could your idea be made simpler? Are there things you could do to the concept to make it more readily understood? Could it be easier to make? Or is there a simpler way to serve this Pain Point?

Are you pushing this idea to prove a point? (Killer Question)

People often say "Success is the best form of revenge," but that is not a good reason to push forward an idea. Revenge is not a Pain Point. Maybe you were told by others your idea would not work and that made you mad. Forget what they say. Judge for yourself. Be successful, but on your BEST idea! Not one with personal grievances attached. "Are you pushing this idea to prove a point?"

Do you have something better than Faster Horses?

Henry Ford is reputed to have said "if I had given them what they wanted they would have had faster horses!" Ford believed so strongly and ignored the market view. If you have a product or service idea that you believe in with every sinew of your body, then put it forward. BUT NOT TO LAUNCH! Put it into the Market Research phase. "Is this a Faster Horses Idea?"

Is one of your ideas hard to love but stands out as profitable?

Many say "do what you love." But maybe you have a Manure Love idea. I argue that if you were paid enough to pick up manure off the road in front of all your friends, naked you would love the business if it made you a millionaire. Is your idea hard to love but profitably serves a real Pain Point? If yes, then move it forward.

SSUP IDEA SCREENING

6.6. Evolution is the final slice of CAKE Idea Screening. The questions poised in the Evolution section are designed to help you think about how ideas might develop. As you will recall from the beginning of the book, the Start Up Safe Sequence is all about finding business ideas and models that allow significant growth and expansion. So the questions make total sense in measuring each of your ideas against their potential to evolve into a great business for you.

Is the idea a business or a job?

This really is one of the top questions in the screening process. Is your idea a glorified job or a true business? Job type self-employment is when you go to work for a fee per job or daily rate, like a plumber or hairdresser. The acid test is when you are ill and cannot work, does any revenue flow in on the days you are in bed. If the answer is NO you are in a job/self-employment. We are looking for ideas where you would have revenue on the days you are ill. It's not a good start up idea if it can't run without you.

Is it a scalable idea?

To be clear, having an idea that will give business growth is NOT the same as scalability. Scalability is really about being able to repeat the same trick, whether it be in a new town/city or online without repeating the majority of costs. The most successful scale ups generally involve technology, so the cost of getting a new client is very small.

Is this idea the cornerstone of a repeatable business model?

A repeatable business idea is really a model. It is about creating such clarity in the minds of customers, employees and even supply chain about what you do and what you stand for that you are able to put multiple ideas through the business and customers still give their support and revenue. Do you have clarity on this? Is this idea the cornerstone of a repeatable business model?

Is it Getoutable?

Getoutable simply means that you can extract yourself from working in the business soon after launch. Can you envisage extracting yourself from day to day activity in sales, operations, finance and hands on activities in the space of 12 months? Is this idea Getoutable?

6.7 IDEA SCREENING QUESTIONNAIRE
START UP SAFE SEQUENCE (SUSS)

C.A.K.E.	Key Questions to Apply to Each of Your Ideas — Yes or No Answers
Clarity	- Is it really a Painkiller or just a Vitamin? Y/N - Avatar –do you see the customer type? Y/N - Will it generate revenue within 90 days in your bank? Y/N - Is it feasible financially to test launch? Y/N
Alignment	- How much knowledge do you have? Y/N - Is this an idea that is close to your interests? Y/N - Do you have a talent linked to this idea? Y/N - Do you have enough experience around this idea? Y/N
Kooky	- Is your idea simple enough? Y/N - Are you pushing this idea to prove a point? Y/N - Do you have something better than Faster Horses? Y/N - Is your idea hard to love but profitable? Y/N
Evolution	- Is the idea really a business or just a job? Y/N - Is it a scalable idea? Y/N - Is this idea the cornerstone of a repeatable business model? Y/N - Is it Getoutable? Y/N

www.bouncepreneurs.com

6.8. Example A. IDEA SCREENING QUESTIONNAIRE with Yes/No response

In this example the entrepreneur decides the idea is not financially feasible as it is too complex and realises that she is not being objective, rather considering this idea to prove a point

C.A.K.E.	Key Questions KQF = Killer Question Fail
Clarity SSUP IDEA SCREENING	• Is it really a painkiller or just a vitamin? (Y/N) • Avatar –do you see the customer type? (Y/N) • Will it generate revenue within 90 days in your bank? (Y/N) • Is it feasible financially to test launch? (Y/N) KQF
Alignment SSUP IDEA SCREENING	• How much knowledge do you have? (Y/N) • Is this an idea that is close to your interests? (Y/N) • Do you have a talent linked to this idea? (Y/N) • Do you enough experience do you have around this idea? (Y/N)
Kooky SSUP IDEA SCREENING	• Is your idea simple enough? (Y/N) KQF • Are you pushing this idea to prove a point? (Y/N) KQF • Do you have something better than Faster Horses? (Y/N) • Is your idea hard to love but profitable? (Y/N)
Evolution SSUP IDEA SCREENING	• Is the idea really a business or just a job? (Y/N) • Is it a scalable idea? (Y/N) • Is this idea the cornerstone of a repeatable business model? (Y/N) • Is it Getoutable? (Y/N)

www.bouncepreneurs.com

6.9. Example B. IDEA SCREENING QUESTIONNAIRE with Yes/No response

In this example the entrepreneur realises he has zero alignment with the idea, in terms of knowledge, interests, his own talent and experience

C.A.K.E.	Key Questions Key Questions KQF = Killer Question Fail
Clarity	<ul><li>Is it really a painkiller or just a vitamin? (Y/N)</li><li>Avatar –do you see the customer type? (Y/N)</li><li>Will it generate revenue within 90 days in your bank? (Y/N)</li><li>Is it feasible financially to test launch?/ (Y/N)</li></ul>
Alignment	<ul><li>How much knowledge do you have? (Y/N) KQF</li><li>Is this an idea that is close to your interests? (Y/N) KQF</li><li>Do you have a talent linked to this idea? (Y/N) KQF</li><li>Do you enough experience do you have around this idea? (Y/N) KQF</li></ul>
Kooky	<ul><li>Is your idea simple enough? (Y/N)</li><li>Are you pushing this idea to prove a point? (Y/N)</li><li>Do you have something better than Faster Horses? (Y/N)</li><li>Is your idea hard to love but profitable? (Y/N)</li></ul>
Evolution	<ul><li>Is the idea really a business or just a job? (Y/N)</li><li>Is it a scalable idea? (Y/N)</li><li>Is this idea the cornerstone of a repeatable business model? (Y/N)</li><li>Is it Getoutable? (Y/N)</li></ul>

www.bouncepreneurs.com

6.10. Summary and Comparison Table for Your 10 Ideas

How to Use
1. Write your idea names in the long space provided. For more than 10 ideas duplicate the table
2. These are all Yes/No questions. Put a Y or an N in each box for each of your ideas. You can total your Yeses at the bottom for clarity.
3. But, Shaded Columns are Idea Killer Questions. If your answer is NO to these, a Killer Question Fail (KQF) then do not to advance it forward.
4. Finally select the 3 best scoring Ideas in order of Yeses and move the No1 Idea to Market Research

Question/Idea	1	2	3	4	5	6	7	8	9	10
Your Idea Name										
Clarity										
True Painkiller										
Seeing Avatar										
Revenue in 90										
Feasible										
Alignment										
Knowledge										
Interests										
Talent										
Experience										
Kooky										
Simple										
Proving Point										
Faster Horses										
Manure										
Evolution										
True Business										
Scalable										
Repeatable										
Getoutable										
Killer Q Fail										
Killer Q Pass										
Total Yeses										

Idea 1	My 1st Idea for the Market Research Stage is
Idea 2	My 2nd Idea to hold in reserve is
Idea 3	My 3rd Idea to hold in reserve is

6.11. What you have learned in this Chapter

In this Chapter you have learned to scrutinise the 10-20 Idea you generated earlier.

You have performed this screening task in an objective, honest and balanced way. Well done – being objective is an important skill used by Professional Entrepreneurs.

Where there are major issues connected to the idea, you have been strong in acknowledging the issue.

Finally you have used this process to select your best 3 ideas. The Number 1 Idea you are taking forward into Market Research, with the 2nd and 3rd best ideas being held in reserve.

Your reserve ideas are important and not there for show. You may be coming back for them.

Now we will progress to the next Chapter on Market Research, where your idea will be further scrutinised and developed.

7. SUSS Market Research

7.1. What You Are Going to Learn in This Chapter

Now we are at the Market Research stage of the Start Up Safe Sequence (SUSS). This is where you begin to see what your idea looks like to other people.

You will learn some traditional and more modern research techniques.

Very importantly, you will think about the critical information targets you need to gather and not simply questions on a questionnaire.

In this Chapter you are going to research your idea and decide if you should progress it. You will:-

a. Follow a simple Market Research plan
b. Test if you have found a true Pain Point
c. Understand the difference between surveys and Information Targets
d. Get a deep understanding of your best customer target group by building a Customer Avatar
e. Learn about market research tools and how to combine them to suit your own needs

7.2. What are Information Targets?

Before you start thinking or designing surveys, think about your Information Targets. INFORMATION TARGETS are the items of information you absolutely must know.

Questionnaire survey tools are now so good, it makes designing surveys easy. Maybe too easy! Too often the layout is beautiful, but the goals of the survey are weak. Like a great CGI movie with a weak plot. Forget about surveys, questions and methods for a minute. Those are just mechanics.

I suggest you need to collect information on **7** Information Targets to assess if your idea has merit. The big one is your CORE INFORMATION TARGET – your idea MUST pass this test! Here it is.

DOES RESEARCH SHOW CUSTOMERS HAVE THE SAME PAIN POINT YOU THINK THEY HAVE?

PLUS you will need to research 6 additional Information Targets, I show how to collect all this below.

1) Their current solution?
2) Market size - How many customers?
3) Their spending power?
4) Demographics of your customer
5) Influencers - What do your customers hear?
6) Location - Where are they?

I explain it all simply and this process WILL work in all scenarios. Some useful terms to know are:-

- Primary research = new information collected by YOU as fresh data you can trust
- Secondary research = existing information that is not new and can be of varying quality
- Quantitative = numbers, Qualitative = feelings, observations or customer behaviours

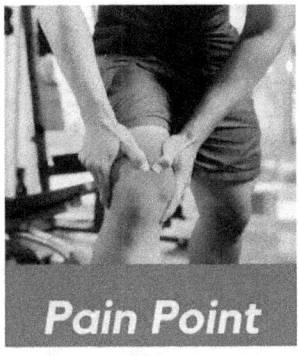

SSUS MARKET RESEARCH

7.3. Pain Point Information Target

To establish whether the Pain Point I am seeing can be confirmed from customers themselves.

Research Methodology

This is your Core Information Target. This information comes directly from customers.

I recommend 5 types of qualitative research to see how customers feel about this Pain Point.

Google search - check if the Pain Point you are describing is being discussed, complained about online. Later in this Chapter we have some tricks to help you get the most out of your search time.

YouTube – look for Life Hacks around this Pain Point. If there are many, you are onto something.

Online Classic customer survey – this will be the main way to deeply understand whether you have found a Paint Point or not. Survey tools like Survey Gizmo and Survey Monkey will serve you well in producing and analysing the questionnaire. They give you links allowing you to issue the survey into multiple channels on social media, in emails, tablets and smartphone texts. You can also get code to drop into your own web page. It is pretty simple to do in site builders and also WordPress themes.

Clipboard version of Classic Customer survey - You can also print the survey and run it at an event where there is a concentration of people in your proposed target market. This lets you can get lots done quickly. This is good for B2B and B2C. These days a tablet is more normal and makes the analysis much easier.

Competitor Sites Examine websites and social media presence to pick up any signs of the PAIN POINT problem or dissatisfaction that your service can resolve.

You do need to profile your respondents by age, sex, income or job type, where they live in your survey design. This will allow you to build a clear picture of your customer Avatar.

Please Note – there is an example survey and guidance notes in the Appendices of the book.

SSUS MARKET RESEARCH

7.4. Current Solution Information Target

To identify in detail what is the customers' current solution to the perceived Pain Point.

Research Methodology

We will of course be able to ask respondents in the survey mentioned above how they are solving Pain Points. But sometimes respondents may be reluctant to answer this openly – especially if it is an Embarrassment Pain Point for example.

So, alternative means will also be needed. There are three main ways of finding out more, firstly Online Information, secondly Expert Opinion and thirdly Focus Groups.

Expert Opinion - Imagine you are an entrepreneur who believes the task of mowing lawns is a Pain Point for senior citizens who can no longer manage their lawnmower. You might set up a meeting, or telephone call with local garden centres and head of their lawn care department. This would be a broad conversation with perhaps just two or three topics

- Does this lawn expert see it as a Pain Point?
- Is it changing what people are buying or behaving?
- What does he think the solution might be?

A word of caution, NEVER rely on the opinion of a single expert. Interview at least 4, before drawing conclusions, sometimes the most confident, credible experts can be very ignorant in terms of developments so beware. But a single expert can say one thing of tremendous value.

Online Hacks - YouTube and Pinterest for workarounds or life hacks that might be highlighting the lack of a mainstream solution for the Pain Point you have identified. Also look at the comments.

Focus Group - you might want to organise a Group with senior citizens. A church group is an idea. Ask 6-8 people along in exchange for a donation to their Church roof appeal or a small gift for each participant. If you can run more than one Group even better!

Classic survey – you simply ask – What are you doing to solve this pain point?

SSUS MARKET RESEARCH

7.5. Market Size Information Target

How big is my market?

Research Methodology

Market size can mean <u>different</u> things and it is important you understand this. If you see a statistic saying the market for hot tub covers is 50 million units this is probably not your accessible market.

- Global Market –total market for your product – example the total global market for hot tub covers.
- You're 365 Day Market – this is the total market you can hope to reach with your business functions fully developed at 365 days from launch. For example the total market for hot tub covers in the UK.
- Launch-able Market – this is a conservative estimate of the percentage of the market you could hope to win given your resources, brand, marketing, sales resources, supply and pricing. This could be the total market for hot tub covers sold direct in South Wales.

If this idea progresses to the Business Modelling stage of the SUSS, then you can also work up how many units or customers you CAN serve from your supply. You may only have a limited supply you see. There will be limits to this of course. This will give you an accurate launch-able market size.

<u>How to Find Market Size</u>

1. Define your customer in around 30 words to the best of your current knowledge, set a few characteristics about the customers in your market – don't forget the Pain Point. For example "Homeowners, who love to entertain, with hot tubs older that two years, which they regularly use for themselves and guests." Use this to start defining the market.

2. The next job is to gather as much information as you can on your market online. I advise that you spend about an hour a day on this for two weeks. If you enter this market, never stop researching by the way. There is always another source!

Data is available in 4 main silos:-

Government data – in the UK this would be the Office of National Statistics, for example. To find your national statistics organisation enter "national bodies for statistics" into Wikipedia for an up to date list. Government data is generally good for big picture understanding and especially demographics. But it is not so strong if you are expecting to find specific data on your product or service market size. But it is still worth investing time, because it often throws up real gems.

Facebook – Facebook provides a great way to make market size estimates. For example, if you were planning a business selling hot tub covers, but you feel you could only manage delivery in Wales to begin with. Facebook's "Create an Ad" tool may help you to size your potential target market. You do this in your Facebook account using "Create an ad". You don't have to pay for an advert, so do not worry, you simply enter dummy information. You have to enter a URL and click "suggest an ad" to start the process. Facebook will ask you for a photograph so get one ready and continue. There are several great targeting options to assist you in zooming in on your specific market of interest. So you can focus on Welsh hot tub owners/people interested in hot tubs within 200 km of your location, giving you a figure of 3,800 people in your target market. Of course this information is only a good as what users tell Facebook, but it is very useful. (This example is for explanatory purposes only).

Paid Reports – there is a huge industry out there supplying "off the shelf" reports to businesses. Organisations like Mintel have a cookie cutter approach to research markets and broad coverage. For technology sectors and new software applications there are organisations like Garner and Ovum. Now for sole entrepreneurs these reports may be financially out of reach. However, you will find summary data online if you dig around. In terms of the general report providers, if you go through your local business support agency and tell them which report you are trying to see, they may have a subscription for the service and can make it available in whole or part. A final word of warning, not all "off the shelf" reports are high quality and price is not always an indicator of accuracy. So never rely on a single source for market sizing.

Competitor Reviews – one way to get market size data is to look for reviews of existing suppliers. This could be Which! Consumer Reports or online comparisons of many products and services. Sometimes the article will report on the size of the market and this can give you a guideline.

Newspaper/Business Magazine Features – quality business orientated newspapers often carry out industry level market profiles. Typically you will find the article online, but only be able to view the first 10 percent. But it may be worth paying a subscription for a month or two to get your hands on a key article. Again it is worth asking your local business advice agency or library if they have a subscription to newspapers that you can use.

Intelligent Estimation – you may find that you do not have a reliable market size data on your specific area of interest. In this case you need to work out a market size calculation yourself. For example, you might be thinking of running a virtual Saturday school for Polish children living in the UK. So you know there are 500,000 5-16 year old children in this category, with 80 percent having access to a smartphone. You also know that 10 percent of Polish families are paying for private healthcare through Polish medical centres in the UK. Now if a family can afford private healthcare it is not a stretch of the imagination to assume they could afford to educate their children in Polish. So this would give you 500,000 x 0.8 x 0.1 = 40,000. That would give you a total market of 40,000. Now this is not a perfect assessment, but sometimes you have to make intelligent assumptions.

SSUS MARKET RESEARCH

7.6. Spending Power Information Target

Can the customers I am targeting afford to spend what I will be charging?

Research Methodology

At this point you may not be entirely certain what you are going to charge for your service. You will be able to fine tune this in the next stage of the Start Up Safe Sequence Business Model. But you should have a fair idea of your price range.

It is straightforward to get pricing on other services and solutions serving your intended customer.

- Check competitive websites to see if the pricing is visible
- Request more information and pricing from competitors
- Ask existing users what they paid for the product/service
- Attend trade shows and pick up physical catalogues or ask competitors about pricing

But you need to know whether your target group can afford your product or service. Always find out the respondents salary of job level to gauge their income. So we would test this in two further ways

- Ask what respondents would be prepared to pay on your classic survey questionnaire
- Look at product reviews , because these often show accurately customer pricing
- Look at eBay and Amazon to see what similar products are selling for. Remember you may be solving the PAIN POINT in a very different way, so it is worth looking at the current widely used solution to the problem and it's pricing.

With pricing data, you can establish if your target customer can afford your solution using competitors pricing. If you intend to price lower or at the same price point as the customer already pay – then they can afford it obviously. If you intend to price above or well above the current price point, no amount of market research will give you an accurate view. Respondents are often reluctant or exaggerate their annual salaries, so go for their job level to gauge income. It is worth a question in your survey, BUT the real test of what customers WILL pay **can only** be validated in a live launch or test launch. **For me this is absolutely a fact!**

SSUS MARKET RESEARCH

7.7. Demographics Information Target

To better understand the demographics of your target customer

Research Methodology

Demographic analysis will give you a better understand the quantity, age, sex and household income of people in specific physical areas. It is <u>also</u> useful to know how many people or households are available for you to serve nationally too. The breakdowns vary depending on how your own national statistical service gathers and presents the data.

Government Data - the availability of free government supplied data varies from country to country. I am using the UK as an example. But in most countries it is free. The following link takes you to a great resource for demographics. It is called Infuse.

https://census.ukdataservice.ac.uk/get-data/aggregate-data

Using the link above you can interrogate census data on the UK for age, sex, income, family structure and many other items. You can also zoom in to county or ward level if you need to. There is a solid explainer video showing how it works. Once you've selected the data you download it in .CSV.

I have used the UK as an example but to find similar services in your country visit the United Nations Index at https://unstats.un.org/home/nso_sites/

Generally there are **five** big variables that can be checked using demographics.

1. Income   2. Household Structure   3. Age   4. Race   5. Education

But I would also suggest you look for data and trends on how things are changing. If you spot a trend in the data it is a good idea to Google your assumption, so if you observed there were fewer small businesses for example, you could search for this and will probably get some good discussion documents on the topic.

SSUS MARKET RESEARCH

7.8. Influencers Information Target

Who are you target customer's influencers?

Research Methodology

This is probably the most challenging of the 7 information targets, because at this stage you do not have relationships with customers to investigate. If you did you could look at their social media activity and draw conclusions.

This puts a great emphasis on asking potential customers who their influences are around their PAIN POINT. You can find out who their influences are in two ways

- Through your Classic survey
- By targeting existing (or recent past) users of product or service in social media

If you search Pinterest on your Pain Point/topics like, it you will find profiles of individuals who you can approach to participate in your survey AND you get a clear view of their interests too.

On Twitter go to organisations serving the type of customer you hope to get. Look for instances of customers responding to tweets linked to your Pain Point, then request to follow these customers and simply ask if they will help you out with some research – your questionnaire The more home spun and small business you make this approach the better, be yourself and be ethical.

But social media is an open playing field so you can find your competitor's Twitter followers by tracking tweets about them and jumping into the tweet exchange. At this point you can explain that you are testing a new concept (not selling) and some of those customers will allow you to survey them. You can also look at their own profiles on Twitter and see what else they are engaging in. Their sex, age, occupation and location can also be gained from this approach. The same goes for Facebook, by checking out your competitors Facebook page, you can see who their followers are and which followers tend to interact the most. You can then target these customers and offer them your survey. Facebook is also a great way to get more information on the demographics of competitor clients as well as their influences using the Lookalike method, which is explained on Facebook.

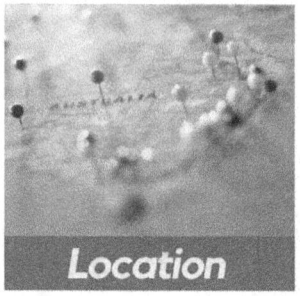

SSUS MARKET RESEARCH

7.9. Location Information Target

Finding a physical location for your business

Research Methodology

If you are planning to start a bricks and mortar business like a restaurant or a garage, that is a business reliant on local customers, you will need to know if they existing in sufficient numbers to hit your sales targets. This is where a location analysis comes in. It prevents you falling in love with a building and locating there without really understanding local customer demand.

The difference between a location and a demographic analysis is simple. Location helps you to pick a site for your business. They both use the same resources, so the two links for Infuse in the UK example and the United Nations stand good.

https://census.ukdataservice.ac.uk/get-data/aggregate-data   Infuse UK

https://unstats.un.org/home/nso_sites/ United Nations list of country statistical resources

Using demographics you can significantly improve the quality of your location decision.

- How many people and sometimes businesses are based in the geography you hope to serve
- How many of these people are close in age, sex, income and other factors to your ideal client
- Whether there is a significantly better location in the vicinity

Example

I once did a study covering two neighbouring towns.

One was considered "poor and rough," the other "rich and refined." My client was planning to launch a jewellery business and had discounted the "poor and rough" town in favour of its "richer" neighbour. But the demographics actually showed that amongst **employed** people the salaries in the poorer town were (on average) higher than in the rich town. Whilst it was true there were a lot more unemployed people in the poorer town, the number of people working and salaried was similar between the two locations. So the client capitalised on less competition and much lower overheads by locating in the poorer town.

7.10. Summary Plan

Below is a summary of the 7 information targets and 7 research tools. Complete this form to make a simple and effective plan for your market research investigation. There is an example survey at the end of this chapter.

My Market Research Plan

CLASSIC SURVEY

CORE INFO TARGET
DOES THE RESEARCH CLEARLY SHOW THE CUSTOMER HAS THE PAIN POINT I THINK THEY HAVE?

FOCUS GROUPS

DEPTH INTERVIEWS

INFO OBJECTIVES

Their current solution

Market size

Spending power

Demographics

Influencers

Location

ONLINE RESEARCH

COMPETITIVE RESEARCH

TRADE EVENTS

OFF THE SHELF RESEARCH

FILL IN
Fill in the number of surveys you plan, deadlines for completion, on and offline sources, events you will attend and experts you will interview

7.11. What you have learned in this Chapter

The most important lesson you have learned in this Chapter is to interact with real people to understand whether you have identified a real Pain Point. This is the core backbone of Choose an Idea and choosing a successful idea.

You now know a lot more about how your idea looks to other people. Plus you know a lot more about the characteristics and prospective customers. Who, what, where and how many

You have learned how to gather the important data you really need, which is based around the 7 Information Targets I have pinpointed for you.

So now you can

- Build and follow a simple research plan
- Really test if you have found a true Pain Point
- Think further about the information targets you need to know and not just throwing questions at people.
- Build an Avatar of what your real customer looks like

If you research has shown you that you have found a real Pain Point that resonates with a good number of people or businesses you should move forward to the next Chapter covering your SUSS Business Model.

You may have discovered that customers are not recognising or confirming your Pain Point. Maybe you have learned the numbers of customers are smaller than you need. Well done I congratulate you.

THIS IS A SUCCESS

Now you must take the Professional Entrepreneur's decision and drop this idea. There is no shame in dropping an idea.

IT IS THE SMART MOVE!

Simply go back to your Idea Screening stage and repeat the process using your second idea. That is the intelligent move. Very well done!

Sample Survey for Identifying a Customer Pain Point

This example is for an IT and Communications professional seeking to identify Pain Points in legal firms. He has an idea that they would pay for a drip feed of training courses on key topics.

Hello my name is Joe Bloggs and I am carrying out genuine market research on IT and Communications issues within legal practices. I have a short survey, there is no selling at all, but your responses could really help me to Choose an Idea for my new business.

1. Generally, how relaxed do you feel about the IT and Communications in your firm? Please tick one answer

a) I think it is well controlled ( )
b) We have few issues but nothing major ( )
c) It is always a challenge to keep up with developments ( )
d) We have some major challenges ( )

2. If you had three wishes to improve IT and Communications in your firm, what would you use them on? Answer in a few of your own words below

Wish 1

_____
_____

Wish 2

_____
_____

Wish 3

_____
_____

3. What is the biggest headache you have in terms of IT and Communications at the moment? Please answer in a few of your own words

Our biggest headache at the moment is

_____
_____

4. How do you deal with this headache at the moment? Please answer in a few of your own words even if it is not a perfect solution.

_____
_____
_____

5. Regarding your IT and Communication challenges which of the following phrases best describes your firm's approach? Please select one answer

a) We go to our contracted IT supplier for help?
b) Our own IT specialist colleagues find a solution internally?
c) We go to various external organisations for help when we need to?
d) Other (please specify)_____

6. Which Sources of Advice and Training do you respect in IT and Communications for Law firms? Please tell us or if there isn't one just write "nobody."

_____
_____

7. If there was a training resource on IT and Communications that you could use to solve most of your own issues and keep you up to date on best practice in legal firms, how interested would you be in subscribing to this service? Assuming it was at an acceptable price. Please select one of the following responses

a) Very interested ( )
b) Interested ( )
c) Not very interested ( )
d) Totally uninterested ( )

8. Is there anything else you think would be useful to know about your firm and IT and Communications that would assist us in helping to serve you and similar legal firms? Please tell us in a few of your own words_____
_____
_____
_____

Finally, would you like to see the results of my survey? If yes please tick the button below and provide your email if you have not already done so.

I wish to see the results of this survey [ ]

My email is _____ @ _____

That is the end of our survey. Many, many thanks for your time today.

Interview Use Only

Respondent Name _____

Respondent Job Title _____

Respondent Email _____

Respondent Tel _____

8. Start Up Safe Sequence Business Model

8.1. What You Are Going to Learn in this Chapter

Congratulations for testing your business idea thoroughly in the Market Research stage of the SUSS. You will be using the Safer Start Up Business Model to plan your business test launch and beyond.

Now you have a Pain Point idea based on a "Bankable Assumption." Here's a good example.

My example is BuildaBear. This business idea sits on the Bankable Assumption that parents would pay quite a lot of money to let their kids buy and dress up a bear in a store. This is a Bankable Assumption that has worked.

> Please hear me at this stage. If you have not done the market research work, or the research did not show a customer that saw your solution as a Pain Point.
> **PLEASE DO NOT GO FORWARD! PLEASE DO NOT GO FORWARD!**

8.2. Start Up Safe Sequence SuSS Canvas

I have designed a single page version of the SUSS Business Model especially for Pain Point based Test Launches. This is called the SUSS Canvas. In this Chapter we will use the SUSS Canvas to examine what you have and also need to move to your Test Launch.

The SUSS Canvas really covers 4 main areas:-

1. Offering – what you have to offer the customer
2. Infrastructure – what you have in place to deliver and serve your customers
3. Customers – knowing who and where they are and how to best reach and serve them
4. Finances – how you will fund this business through the test phase, full launch and beyond

This SUSS Canvas is a single sheet which shows 9 building blocks for your business.

These are:-

1. Pain Point – a simple statement of the Pain Point you have proven in the Market Research Phase
2. Bankable Solution – your solution which you believe customers with your Pain Point will buy
3. Single Customer – the details of the customer Avatar you will be targeting and selling to.
4. Test Launch Model – creating a scalable product/service for little money to prove the idea
5. Key Partners – your key suppliers, channel partners and agencies supporting your launch
6. Tribe – how to stop competition copying you, by leading a Tribe and starting a Movement
7. Income 30/60/90 – this is the source/s of revenue you will get paid in the first 30/60/90 days
8. Spend 30/60/90 – these are you main cost/s of launch you have to pay in days 30/60/90
9. Key Tasks and Metrics – these are the tasks that must succeed and your key measurements

A blank copy of the single sheet SUSS Canvas follows. I suggest you print out several copies and use a pencil, because it will take a few goes to get it ready.

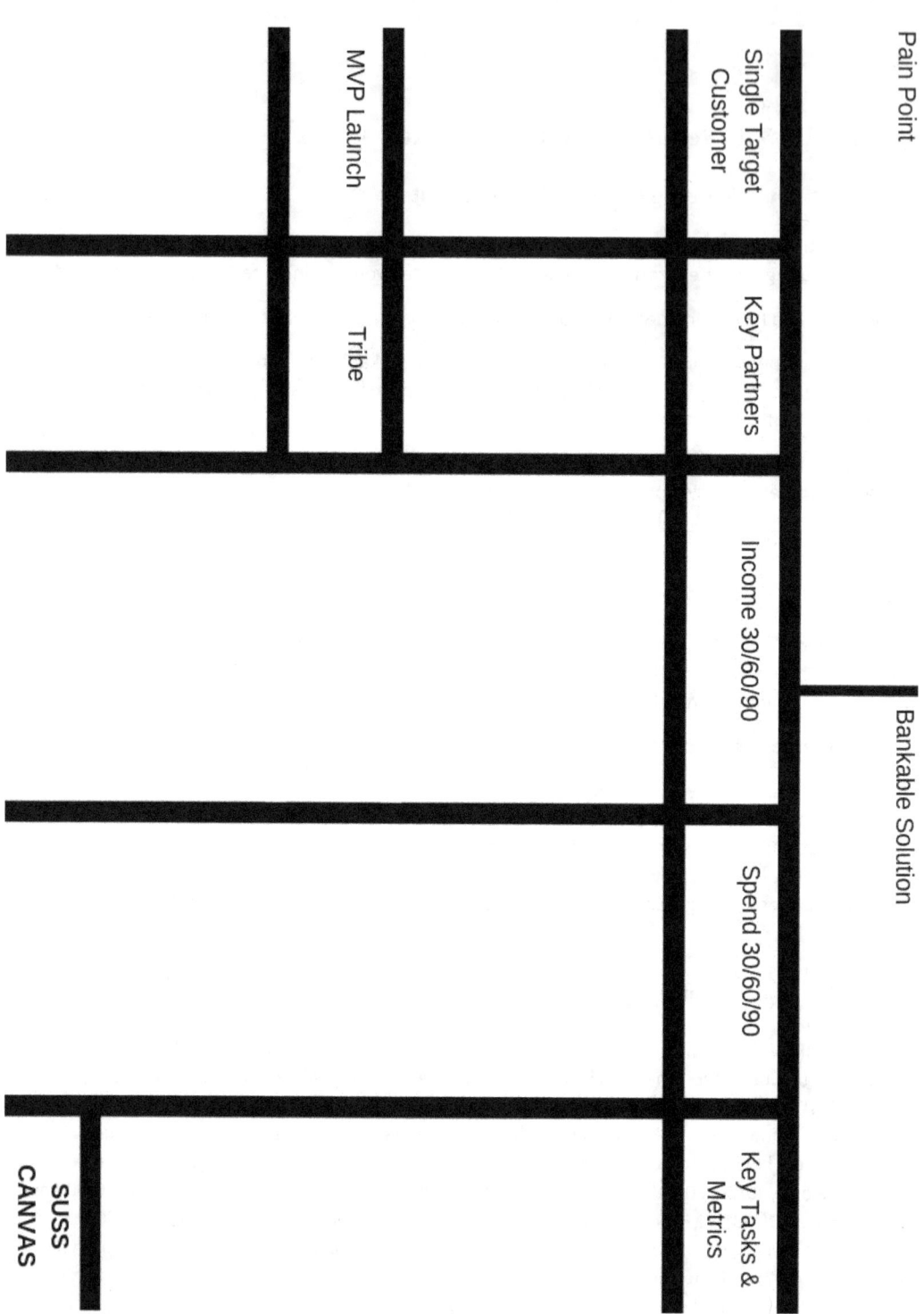

See www.chooseanidea.com for downloadable version.

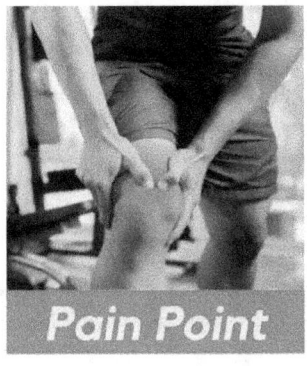

SUSS CANVAS

8.3. Description – Pain Point

By now you will know what a customer Pain Point is. But here is my definition for you.

1. Specific customer type
2. Clear Pain rather than discomfort
3. A supply opportunity that is Scalable and Repeatable
4. Serving this Pain Point will allow you to build a business you can work on rather than a job you can work in.

Tasks on the SUSS Canvas

1. Simply state the Pain Point you will be addressing
2. Do this in no more than 10 words
3. Do not state the solution.
4. Just the Pain Point being felt NOT the solution

Examples

Infestation of buildings by wasps, ants or bees.

Waiting weeks for replacement covers making hot tubs unusable

Lack of direction in life

Constant need to replace charger cables for mobile phone

Unable to write book due to constant distractions

Time taken to commute to the gym

Crooked teeth unable to afford cosmetic dentistry

Having no access to the internet

That's all you have to do on the Canvas – write in the Pain Point you will be addressing – and then you are done.

SUSS CANVAS

8.4. Description – Bankable Solution

Your Bankable Solution is your specific solution to the Pain Point you have found. We call it your Bankable Solution because it is guaranteed to

Ease The Customer's Pain AND Guarantee your Bankable Revenue

And this will be tested in the real market in your Test Launch.

Tasks on the SUSS Canvas

In the Bankable Solution box you really need to pin point your solution to the Pain Point. This is not a place for "flim flam."

Again just 10 words.

Your description has to clearly state how you will resolve the customer's Pain. This is the basis for your whole launch, investment, time and confidence.

It needs to be good. In fact, it must be very good and testable in the real market.

Examples

We will remove flying insect nests within 24 hours

Specialist male camp to rebuild life direction

Our hot tub covers are delivered to your door in a maximum of 72 hours

We provide a guaranteed for life phone charger

Writer's retreat provides the perfect environment to finish your book

Our home gym removes wasted time commuting to the gym

Affordable at home treatment changing crooked teeth into winning smiles

Think hard about your Bankable Solution. Make sure it is simple and clearly understandable to yourself AND customers. Ask people around you what it means to them and adjust accordingly.

SUSS CANVAS

8.5. Description – Single Target Customer

This is where you summarise the specific type of customer you are aiming for. You need absolute clarity in this for your Test Launch. This dictates your marketing, your sales approach also many of your key tasks and metrics. Be precise.

Tasks on the SUSS Canvas

The Single Target Customer box on your SUSS contains five spaces for you to clearly identify the characteristics of your Single Target Customer. You need to be precise filling these in. In the example below you see two descriptions for the hot tub cover example.

Hot Tub Cover Example Single Target Customer Examples	
Loose Description	Tight Description
Homeowner	Existing Hot Tub Owner
Age 25-65	Age 28+
Male or Female	Couples
Income above 30,000 per annum	Blue collar workers
Interested in Home Improvement	Physically active workers

We can see that in the Tight Description the customer is qualified as already owning a hot tub. The age group is not artificially narrow and allows anyone from 28 years and over to be targeted. Most hot tubs are bought by couples and this is reflected. But in this tight example, market research showed this example entrepreneur that hot tub owners were often blue collar workers, doing physically active work, like nurses, carers, self-employed construction workers and drivers. They enjoyed the hydrotherapy benefits of the hot tub.

Example: Here is another example for the insect nest removal business

1. Customer based in or within 10 miles of the city
2. Customer sees it as acute problem needing attention same day
3. Customer makes token card payment when accepting the service before the call out
4. Customer agrees minimum call out fee during enquiry
5. Customer is the homeowner and will pay on day of service

Try this a few times in rough before completing the five boxes in full.

SUSS CANVAS

8.6. Description – Test Launch

In this part of the SUSS Canvas you will be describing how you plan to test launch your product or service WITHOUT full scale investment. Remember, there is nothing wrong with failing on a business idea. It is better than taking a year of your life and all your savings to find out it is a bad idea the hard way. But you have done the hard work on the Start Up Safe Sequence, so your chances of success are much higher than the typical start up entrepreneur.

Tasks on the SUSS Canvas

What you never do at Test Launch is make the full investment in product manufacture, premises, stock, employees, vehicles, web design or coding that you would do if you were launching a business the traditional way. Complete the box, briefly describing how you will Test Launch.

"TO TEST WHETHER REAL CUSTOMERS IN YOUR TARGET GROUP WILL ACTUALLY BUY FROM YOU!"

Examples

Writer's Retreat	Put your first retreat into a third party hotel, marketing it as a pilot (offer it as a discount in exchange for feedback and people will come)
Software product	Mock up your screens without code. Offer it as available from future date and take part payment while you build the code. If you get enough customers of course!
Online shop	Take photos of products from other stores, with owner's permission and buy from them during test launch (Zappos did this with shoes)
Products you need to show	Use 3D printing to make mock-ups for pitches, photo and video for sites and literature
Physical shop	Get a pop up shop rental for 3 months. Only stock your lead items. Do not fill with expensive stock. If you sell out, you've proven your model
Restaurant	Go to a fete, carnival, Kermesse or other celebration day in the town or city you plan to be in. Offer key items from your menu from a popup stand. See if you can sell them.

We will do more on the Test Launch in the next Chapter.

SUSS CANVAS

8.7. Description – Key Partners

In this section you will pinpoint your key partnerships. Generally good partnerships should do one of three things for you.

1. Make it easier to get key skills or resources you need to succeed at advantageous cost
2. Reduce risk or uncertainty of entering a market
3. Provide energy through a team ethic and clearly shared goals

Sometimes to a key partner you may be one of millions of small customers. This could be true for example if you were using Shopify for e-commerce. You have invested time, effort and money to align your business with their model, so for <u>you</u> they are a key partner.

Being able to socialise with individuals does not make them a key partner and that is for certain. If you are spending long hours alone, "push starting the truck" that is a new business, you may really welcome seeing a friendly face. But that is not enough for Key Partner status.

All partnerships should be based around commercial value to your growing business.

Tasks on the SUSS Canvas

You need to ask the following questions:-

<u>Who are our Key suppliers?</u> – Identify them by name in the box. Note these are not people you buy A4 paper from. Those suppliers are easily replaced and not key suppliers.

<u>Why are they Key Suppliers?</u> - Key Suppliers give you specialist services that are vital to your service and not easy to replace or replace quickly. Record this in the box also

<u>Who are our Key Partners?</u> – that are vital to our business but do not provide paid goods and services. This could include a mentor or business support agency? Again name who they are and why they are a key partner.

Examples

- Management of incubator providing great working space, low cost connections and free extras.
- Welding company supplying your product, allowing you to have safety and quality certification
- Distributor marketing your product, bundling it into a gift box, extending your product range.

SUSS CANVAS

8.8. Description - Tribe

Much is made of Unique Selling Proposition or Unfair Advantage to give you a competitive edge. In reality it is very hard for a Start Up to gain a defendable competitive advantage for long. But you CAN build an advantage over all your competitors and keep them out of your market by creating a very strong tribal mentality amongst customers.

By solving the Pain Point of a specialist group, you can be a leader of a Movement not a business. Your customers will favour you over and over again. This is a TRIBE. Seth Godin brilliantly describes these ideas in his book Tribes, which I thoroughly recommend. His definition is:-

"a group of people connected to one another, connected to a leader, and connected to an idea."

Even if you have a product feature that makes your product unique and protect it commercially, the pace and ferocity of global competition may catch you very quickly indeed. But lead a Tribe or Movement and you will stay ahead. If you combine understanding of the Movement with a great standard of customer service – where you simply offer such a vastly superior customer service you will further lead your tribe.

This works really well if you address the Pain Point first and work so fast to establish yourself that competitors cannot match your coverage. This is typical in online with Airbnb a great example.

If you make yours a tribal marketing approach, building and leading a Movement, you will find yourself with an extremely loyal customer or tribe. This ties in well to Pain Points as it is a latent market that has not been served properly before and people will love you for solving their pain.

Tasks on the SUSS Canvas

Consider which Movement your Pain Point is connected to write this down in the Tribe Box

- Write down the emotional connection between yourself and your followers (customers)
- Write down 3 things you will do to Create and Lead this Movement

Examples

Club Mascots (company making Mascot Suits)	Failed Entrepreneurs (suppling training)
Give them Recognition and Respect	Give them Recognition and Respect
Create a training scheme	Create a bounce back guide
Hold a national convention	Lobby for revised credit rating methods

SUSS CANVAS

8.9. Description – Income 30/60/90

This section on the SUSS covers income coming from the sale of your product or service which is serving your targeted Pain Point customers. Remember Test Launch is primarily about proving demand.

Tasks on the SUSS Canvas

In this section there are four tasks to perform and record in the box.

1. Record the type of sale or sales you intend to make, using the categories below

- Asset sale – simple sales online or offline where ownership transfers for money
- Consumption – charged on the sales of food, drink
- Time Based -nights stayed, days hired, minutes of use, per wash for example
- Subscription - selling continuous access online game, app use, gym membership
- Percentage Brokerage – credit card user fees, post and packaging profit
- Advertising - fees from online like YouTube, pay per click and referrals
- Lending/Renting/Leasing tool hire, garage space rental, letting property
- Licensing – allowing third parties to use your idea, TV programme or brand for a license

2. Set Down You Pricing Framework – fill in the box with your product sales price. If you are selling multiple products this may not viable in our small box (so set out your overall profit margin goals). Remember you will be testing if customers are prepared to pay what you are asking to have their Pain Point relieved. That is the key purpose of your Test Launch.

3. Set Out Your Method of Payment – how you will be taking payment

4. Your revenue sales target for Day 30, 60 and 90 – Write monthly not cumulative targets*

Example	Hot Tub Cover	Duvet Washing Service
Type of Sales/Sales	Asset Sale/Percentage Brokerage	Time
Pricing framework	Small 199/Medium/399/Large 499 Postage 50% mark up	Single 10/Double 20/King+30
Payment Method	PayPal or Credit Card with Order	Full payment or 50:50 deposit/collect card or cash
Revenue Target 30/60/90*	30 = 2k/60 = 5k/90=10k	30 = 2k/60 = 4k/90=8k

SUSS CANVAS

8.10. Description – Spend 30/60/90

This section on the SSUC covers spending to serve your targeted Pain Point customers. At this stage test the costs of actually operating, promoting and selling to live customers. Whilst you may get some sales income before the formal Test Launch starts, you will DEFINITELY incur costs before you launch your business. So the box shows four milestones - Prelaunch/30/60/90

This exercise will help you to figure out

1. The timing of spending both before and after your launch
2. The most important costs in operating this business longer term
3. The key activities that are going to be most expensive
4. What key equipment you HAVE to purchase or rent to run this business
5. What payment terms you should expect from your suppliers

Tasks on the SUSS Canvas

Think about marking your expenditure based on when you have to spend it. Is it a prelaunch spend? Or at Day 30 60 or 90. Consider supplier payment terms as you may be able to use equipment for a period without paying for it. Just make sure you have the reserves to do so, whether you sell or not!

Example Up-front costs

- Test Launch Product/Service Mock ups or Basic Product Range
- Marketing/Sales Support Material
- Software licenses and subscriptions
- Labour support (web site design)

Example After Launch Running Costs

- Marketing and PR costs
- Cost of Sales (transport, pitch materials)
- Supplies of materials or finished product
- Drawings/Salary -you need to take this
- Essential equipment purchase or hire
- Premises (short term)

SUSS CANVAS

8.11. Description – Key Tasks and Metrics

This is the last element of the Safer Start Up Canvas. Here we collect the Key Tasks and Metrics you will need to monitor your venture during Test Launch.

Tasks on the SUSS Canvas

Product Performance	Supplier Success
• Customer feedback on product performance against Pain Point	• Effective Supply • Supplier Issues • Availability
Marketing Success	Spend
• Marketing Quality Success • Marketing Reach • Effectiveness of Lead Generation • Establishment of Tribe	• Adherence to budget • Extra spending areas • Unused budget
Sales Metrics	Service Satisfaction
• Pitches • Conversions • Sales Value • Purchased by anticipated customer type	• Customer satisfaction • Preferred service channels email/phone/chatbot/app
Customer Response to Product	
• Seeing Pain Point • Objections • Reaction to Pricing	

8.12. What you have learned in this Chapter

Working on this Canvas may be alerting you to challenges and cause you to think again or improve the delivery of this idea. You can still go back to Idea Generation and bring forward your second idea. Or keep this idea and strengthen suppliers, marketing or even pivot to another customer type. Importantly you key metrics needed to run and measure success of your business idea.

In the next Chapter you'll learn about all about your Minimum Viable Product Test Launch.

9. SUSS Test Launch - Minimum Viable Product Launch Explained

9.1. What You Are Going to Learn in This Chapter

This Chapter covers the SUSS Test Launch of your new product of service as a Minimum Viable Product (MVP). MVP has many imitators but it is still the best method for solo or small team/resource entrepreneurship. I recommend you read Chapters 9, 10 and 11 together.

You will be guided through a 90 day MVP launch of your new product or service which is intended to offer you the lowest financial and time risk, based on your business model from the previous Chapter. I will show you how to spend 90 days launching your new business idea.

You will also be shown the 4 BIG challenges you will have to overcome to move the business from the first 30 days, leading to a successful first 90 day launch and beyond.

You will also learn that now is the time for you to start changing your approach and thinking more with a sales mentality going forward. No matter how much market pull there is for your idea it will need to be sold AND **you** will be the one doing the selling. There is no doubt that some great ideas fail due to not enough sales energy AND some poor ideas succeed because of very good selling.

Might I remind you as a highly professional entrepreneur you still need to be certain that your venture is DEFINITELY GOING TO WORK! If despite all your testing the idea does not take off, you must ensure you do not lose big in terms of time or cash. You can avoid this by means of this Minimum Viable Product Model. (MVP)

- You will launch your new idea with explosive energy of course. But also with you spending as little money as possible during live testing your business venture.
- In this Chapter you will find out with certainty whether what you're building is something people want by testing it as a live business.
- If it works – you will be prepared to ramp it up into a full business.
- If it comes close you can pivot, make some changes and relaunch
- If it does not sell you must pull out.

<u>Avoid, Avoid, and Avoid the Old Way of Launching a Business</u>

You have already learned NOT to launch your idea the Old Way. The Old Way of launching a business is in fact ridiculous. Think about it, entrepreneurs completed their huge irrelevant business plan, used up lots of energy doing so and the plan had virtually nothing to do with running their actual business. Please do not slip back to this old way of thinking. Stick with the SUSS approach.

The Old Way was great for banks, accountants, lawyers and property agents, but was terrible for start-up entrepreneurs with limited capital. Too many people are ploughing in investment too early in the process that your product testing does not justify. Don't go this way. Don't commit to a full LAUNCH of your new business on Day 1. In the past model you may have done these things:-

- Rented an office, shop or factory
- Bought capital equipment
- Recruited staff
- Sunk in all your savings or borrowed from the bank

Remember failure, using this method can only waste your time, money, credit rating and confidence.

9.2. MVP A Better Way

Nobody wants a failed project

That is why you must sell to a pre-specified target in your first 90 days!

It is better to limit the duration of your launch phase to 90 days. If it works out you go forward. If the venture fails you revert back to earlier SUSS stages. You may need to pivot, modifying your idea or restarting with a totally different idea from the SUSS Idea Screening phase.

I suggest this for three main reasons

1. To minimise your investment in taking your product to market
2. To allow you to know within 90 days whether you have a hit or not
3. To show that you can build a test process that is not just a light bite test of your idea, but it can morph into become your full business roll out within 90 days if it generates sufficient working capital.

The 90 Day Phase is so valuable to entrepreneurs because many of you are boot-strapping or starting up on a shoe-string budget. This approach encourages the most basic, low cost form of the product you can possibly launch.

The idea of trying a "Light Bite" version of a full product before committing resources to full blown launch, is not new - Housebuilders been doing it for years, "buying off plan" as it is called is commonplace. Especially so if the properties are going to be in high demand. Often when houses or especially apartments/flats are built the developer will market the properties to potential buyers before the first home is even started.

If nobody wants to buy, the *build*er does not build. The concept is that simple.

Vendors use computerised and real models to demonstrate what the property might look like and provide samples for floor tiles, kitchen layouts and paint schemes.

So why can't you do this with your product or service?

<u>6 Myths about MVP</u>

1. Steve Blank created MVP as a simple FREE concept to help small entrepreneurs. It is as useful today as when it was created. Criticism of it comes mainly from very large enterprises and consulting firms that have totally different issues to the small entrepreneur.
2. It has been said that MVP leads to product or service designs that are too lean and you will be embarrassed by them. I think that is a concept "cooked up" in a PR-obsessed multi-national that has no wit regarding the "street-fighting" mentality needed to launch your own business.
3. It is proposed that the market has now evolved so far that it will only accept fully evolved products at launch stage. I do see some evidence of this in software designs, but the mock up industry in software has also evolved significantly. Outside of software it's not a valid point.
4. Criticism of MVP ignores the fact that early adopters enjoy being the first to buy new ideas.
5. It also ignores the concept of tribal followings (as highlighted by the great Seth Godin); Tribes like to see someone solve their Pain Point problem in a way that no other organisation has bothered to do before.
6. Finally some suggest that MVP is NOT about selling the design as it stands, that somehow MVP launches are about never-ending tweaks of the product. This viewpoint shows a lack of understanding of the core concept of MVP. <u>MVP is about selling what you have!</u>

9.3. The 6 Launch Rules?

You have to do 6 things to deliver this launch:-

1. You have to build the most basic/low cost version of your product or service you can.
2. You have to commit to a specific launch date and 90 day period without fudging it.
3. You must remember you are doing this to find out IF customers will ACTUALLY buy it as a solution to your Pain Point.
4. You are not market researching, or going to tweak features to get the sale, but get customers to buy it as it stands. Will they buy what you have NOW? Is the key question.
5. If they won't buy what you have now, but make suggestions on what needs to change in order for them to buy it. Record this carefully.
6. Do not discount to get sales, stick to the price point you have planned.

FURTHER CONSIDERATIONS

- Offer a product that you are able to demonstrate in full to the point of asking for money
- It must work or appear to work for demonstration purposes
- It has to be bought within 90 days by a predetermined number of customers
- You need a marketing strategy to complement the launch
- It has to be bought right now. Promises of purchase in the future do not count. Binding orders and payment only.
- Does the customer like it?
- The customer sees it solves the Pain Point problem you designed it for
- The customer loves your product and buys it, but to solve a different Pain Point problem than you envisaged. This is a win if customers consistently buy for this reason
- Is it seen as a better solution to the customer's problem than anything else they have used before?
- Are you getting a lot of sales from a customer group totally different to the one you are targeting?
- It must be a better solution to the customer's problem otherwise you will not build a following
- Build the business plan as a web site
- Remember you don't have to sell it to everybody
- Remember some people who never buy it even if you Gold Plate it and offer it for free
- Have your marketing and operations ready to go and ramp up at a moment's notice.
- A single idea – no customisations for individual customers – no matter how tempting

9.4. How to Build a MVP

Some Ways to Build a Minimum Viable Product (MVP)

There are several ways to build a MVP.

Video Explainer - You simply make a video explainer. This can be done very inexpensively now and you capture sales orders or sales enquiries at the end of the video.

Early Adopter Exclusivity - If you are supplying a fairly big ticket market with perhaps 10 competitors you offer your new product to just three for one year. You present a mock up but say that you will only be working with three "Foundation Partners."

This is especially useful if you sell internationally. You have your anchor clients to use as sales case studies but in every other country you sell to all the customers. In the second year you do the same in your local market.

Concierge - In this model you basically promise the customer a service and then once they have ordered you do all the work needed yourself to ensure they get the service they are paying for. Now you would kill yourself doing this for any length of time, but to prove the concept, it is a good approach.

Wizard of Oz - In the Wizard of Oz a frail old man made outsiders believe he was huge, powerful and almost Godlike with all sorts of trickery.

Well you can do the same projecting a bigger version of your business than you actually are – be careful not to lie. Lying is bad business and bad Karma.

Restricted Product or Service - Offer a "Basic" version of your product. One which you can make or provide easily. Then later you can add whistles and bells and increase the price.

Obviously very popular in software, but it can be used in hospitality, furniture businesses and even car washing.

3D Printed - 3D printing allows manufacturing minded entrepreneurs to build one off examples of what they have in mind for customers. These can be photographed or shown as videos or physically shown to customers to handle.

You can go to 3D printers without buying your own device for one off designs. It is a great idea to launch products.

You Show an Existing Competitors Product - You can show a competitors product and point out deficiencies it has. You can show customers how you have improved on these deficiencies and that the customer can buy this improved version from you now.

Scale Mock ups - You might use 3D printing for this too. Alternatively if you were planning to build a fairground ride for example you could build a scale replica to close the order on. Remember you do not need the full size product to seal your first deals.

Payable Demo - Here you are really selling the idea. You are saying you can see the idea we have, but you must pay to be in the room and sign a non-disclosure agreement (NDA). This raises expectation and interest.

This can be tricky and impossible in my view if you are selling to government. But if you have a radical idea it can be done.

I have seen it done in packaging where customers were told that there would be limited supply for a year, but a new product would cut costs VERY significantly for the customer. Because some of these customers were known to be loyal to competitors, a payable demo and NDA was insisted on. It worked very well, because the supplier was genuinely able to deliver huge savings and the customers were curious and receptive to fixing a problem that no one had yet fully solved.

9.5. Make Buying From You Easy

You may have a great product or service. You have found a need and have a solution the customer wants. But do not make buying difficult for the customer! Bear these points in mind.

Very Simple to Buy – A common mistake that can kill a launch venture is making the e-commerce or simple payment process too complicated. The customer wants to buy, but you cannot take credit cards or you cannot accept an invoice – that is never going to work. Thankfully the fintechs are coming to the rescue with very low test payment terminals. Set something reasonable up, it is worth it and what Professional Entrepreneurs do.

Keep it Simple – Do not bring a complex idea to market. Make sure customers are able to understand it VERY, VERY easily.

No Handcuffs - offer a service that customers can leave if they wish. Do not try to create contractual conditions that are long and very binding. If a customer thinks they can leave easily then they are far more likely to relax and buy.

Try able – just make sure the customer can try the product really easily. Do not make them perform tricks just to get a chance to try it. They will not thank you for it.

Longevity – try to make the product or service you are offering more than just a one deal wonder. Find ways to entice the customer to stay with you for a long time.

9.6. FAQ's

Question – What are the potential outcomes of a MVP test launch?

There are three potential outcomes which I will explain in detail later but for now

Ramp Up – customers in your Avatar buy for your Pain Point reason you ramp up the business

Pivot – it shows some promise, but there are issues so you make a change and try a second launch

Drop – Nobody wants to buy it, the Pain Point does not manifest. Drop it, revisit alternative ideas

Question – What if it does not work out in 90 days?

- If you REALLY feel a small change can make all the difference you modify and try again, but for no more than an additional 30 days
- If the idea doesn't work you abandon it entirely at the end of the 90 days and go back to your alternative ideas

It is better to fail fast; because your launch is MINIMALISTIC you will not waste time and money.

Question – What if it really takes off?

You need to have the process, job roles and tasks to deliver set up in advance.

If it takes off you must be "ready to roll" and handle the volume

Question – What timescales are you recommending?

- You have 90 days from Day 1 of launch to sell this product or service.
- If you cannot sell it to point of cash payment or purchase order the launch has failed.
- If you really feel an adjustment will see this idea lift off then give the venture 30 more days. But do not carry on with the venture if you do not see revenue. Don't do it!
- Take no more than 90 days to prepare for launch. If it takes longer something's wrong

Question – How Should I Demonstrate My Product or Service

You have to be able to demonstrate your product effectively from Day 1 of launch

This can be a physical product, but can also be a simulation ranging from a CAD mock-up, non-functioning website, video presentation or scale model. 3D printing really opens up this method.

Your demonstration is a sales demonstration – pure and simple – you are there to close on this product sale.

You must make certain money promised to you in sales hits your bank account. Until it is in your bank it does not count.

Question – How Much Variation Should I Offer

The short answer is as little as possible.

You should not accept orders for one off variations, design modifications for single customers. If you do this you are winning one sale at the cost of proving your business model.

Keep any ranges you need as limited as possible. Ideally a range of 1 type!

Question – Is it Ethical to Offer a Product You Cannot Deliver?

You must be able to deliver the product or service you have demonstrated and taken money for.

To do anything else is not ethical.

Now it might take you a while to deliver, but so long as you have not duped or misled the customer this is ok.

Quite a few people in retail and B2B markets enjoy being early adopters very much indeed!

Question – How Much Money Should I Spend On This

AS LITTLE AS POSSIBLE. You must build this launch version based on what you can afford. It may just take your time and computer.

It may take other resources that you have at your disposal.

You must think micro budget.

Do not deplete your resources on building sophisticated prototypes. If your idea needs £50,000 to build, find a way of mocking it up virtually.

Do not blow all your savings. Be a Professional Entrepreneur, you may need to abandon this idea and try another if the test costs are more than you can bear.

Question – How do I Judge a Successful Launch?

You must make a salary by the end of your second launch month. It may not be a big salary but you must make one.

You must see that month 3 is going to pay you well and it is time to ramp up fully.

Question – Do I Look for Investors or Take Out a Bank Loan

No you do not. You do not look for investors on your first venture business. You may do this on your second or third venture. But ideally you will self-fund you next business from this one.

If your business idea demands external investment from the start, don't do it. Go back to your ideas and come up with a more modest plan.

Remember your first business needs to be a hit. It is better for it to be successful and small, than unsuccessful and big.

Many more conservative voices will scare you into believing that you cannot launch a business without capital from them. They repeat ad nausea that you should be scared of:-

- Legal Issues
- Fear of Idea Theft
- Fear of Rejection

But get the revenue flowing and take it from there. Investors are easier to find after a successful launch, than when you have not proven the concept.

If you spend a small amount to check the validity of an idea you try another idea. If you invest heavily and it fails – well you are broke with bad credit and that will hurt!

Question – Do I have to wait for Day 1 before Starting Sales and Marketing?

No get going. You must give yourself every advantage you possible can.

- You need a website able to support your sales messages. This must be ready on Day 1.
- Start telling people in your target market about your new product before you launch it
- Build expectation for your product
- You must be able to take payments early in case customers want to buy early and pay you.
- Your website must be able to handle payments, get working on this –again before launch

Question – How much preparation do I need to do for the business really taking off?

A lot is my answer!

- This is a rolling start business. That means you must have a ramp up plan ready
- You need to be prepared to rapidly fulfil orders, outsource non-essentials and build product
- You have to have your processes and the beginnings of job descriptions for your first employees ready.

Question – How good must the quality of my product be?

- Your product or service must be the most basic design you can come up with capable of supporting an ethical sale.
- The quality of your product (although simple) must be good
- You will be able to quickly improve the quality and polish of your product once sales start

Question – How much of a research versus sales process is this?

My advice is simple. It is predominantly a sales process.

Let me emphasize that if you go into a product launch without a total commitment to closing business you are in deep trouble. So:-

- Put on your sales hat
- Come with your A sales game
- Be ready to hustle for business

You will HOWEVER, be able to get other useful information on customer preference.

Question – Should one not think of this as a Research Exercise?

Bear in mind this process can give you great understanding of your customer AND give you a great launch OR it can give you a great understanding of your customer AND save you lots of time and expense if it does not launch well. So there is a research element too.

Question – In What Situation Should I Change My Product "on the Hoof?"

Most successful businesses see a Pivot Point necessity during or shortly after launch. Let me be clear, there is a BIG difference between the odd customer wanting bespoke customisations and a majority of customers showing a need for a revised product.

I suggest the following approach.

If one person asks you to change your product this is a customisation. Two customers ask, then this is still a customisation to be avoided. But if a big chunk of people you try to sell to, keep asking for the same modification, then you should do it. If you know you can make this change, then change your mock up or demo and sell it with the change.

Make it happen. But the Golden Rule is to close the deal, even using the initial design.

"I will change it if you buy it now." Is a good mantra. Here is a real example.

A start up Entrepreneur called Martina manufactured samples of toddler clothes and tried to sell them to the mums she knew from her local kindergarten and playgroups in her area. This lady was from Slovakia. She had used complex hand wash only trimmings, which were traditional and liked in her home country.

But she now lived in the UK and tastes were very different. Many prospective buyers said to her that if the fabrics were more washable they would buy. So Martina decided to Pivot and made up some miniature samples of her clothes from washable fabrics. She sold them alongside her original ornate garments – explaining they were available in washable fabrics too. After she could see this was more popular and people were actually buying she went back to her sewing machine. Like Cinderella she worked really hard to make the same garments in the requested fabrics. This time they sold and they sold really well. In fact they were so successful she was asked by her local nursery Kindergarten to provide these as the official uniform for pre-schoolers.

Martina then made a second Pivot, taking the idea of Kindergarten uniforms to other pre-schools. Now her core business is making washable pre-school children's uniforms for Kindergartens.

Question – What if I Simply Cannot Find Enough Customers in 30 Days

If you have not pitched the product or service to at least 10 customers in your target market with the issue you seek to solve, you have not completed a successful launch. Either because your sales and marketing effort has lacked bite OR...

You may have not completed your market research work properly and you never did have enough customers to support your idea at all. Most likely it is your sales and marketing.

Question – What about a "Failed Launched"

Can I say there is no such thing as a failure in this process. As Professional Entrepreneurs you have test marketed professionally and found the opportunity is not strong enough to proceed.

Well done you have saved yourself a year of your life and probably thousands in cash.

Your launch has failed, but you have succeeded in terms of safeguarding yourself from a potentially ruinous venture. Plus you still have your Number 2 and Number 3 idea to fall back on AND the finance to try another MVP launch.

9.7. You Are Unable to Sell Your Product or Service – DROP

Firstly if the launch does not work out pull the product launch at the end of 90 days. You have to retreat and rethink.

Be sure to contact all customers who you have taken or progressing orders with and explain openly and honestly what has happened. Refund all monies not owed to you. Apologise sincerely for the inconvenience. People are amazing in these situations. It is important to do this because the same people may become your customers for a revised product launch in the future.

I encourage you to remember 4 key things.

- You are acting as a Professional Entrepreneur NOT a Failure
- The learning will allow you to go back to the earlier SUSS Stages and be even more Professional in your approach
- You have saved a huge amount of time, effort and money compared with a less organised venture launch. You have progressed.
- Do not be downbeat – you've done well – although you may of course be disappointed.

If the launch fails, think like a Professional Entrepreneur not an Amateur Entrepreneur. Once you become a serial Entrepreneur you will accept some failure in product launch as part of the process.

So pull the product and review the experience carefully.

If you feel there is merit in a rebuild of your product, take it back to Market Research. You may decide there is some opportunity worth salvaging OR you should totally abandon the idea.

Idols- a special message for you! If it has failed let it go.

9.8 What if the Business Really Takes Off? – Ramp Up

A good way of thinking is like a survival expert such as Bear Grylls, Laura Zerra or Ray Mears. They all prepare very carefully when lighting a fire.

- With care they find tinder just a tiny amount of inflammable material.
- A pre-prepared pile of very thin twigs sits right next to them.
- Next to these are slightly bigger twigs. Then a few big branches.
- They carefully rub sticks together to get a spark on the tinder.
- Once the smallest flames appear in their tinder, they blow on the fire, but then come the small pre-prepared twigs right next to them, which they can reach straight away.
- When these light on go the next biggest twigs, again very close by – pre-prepared.
- And then when the fire is established on go the big logs. Yes these are there pre-prepared too.
- Once the tiny spark catches fire, do these experts have to find some small twigs? No. They are ready.
- When the small twigs are alight does he go off to get some branches? Again No. They are ready. AND so must you when your idea catches light. You must have everything right next to you to make it work immediately.

9.9. What if there is demand but I see the need to change – PIVOT

Firstly you should never use a Pivot as an excuse for extending a failed MVP launch. So it is important that I set out clear guidance for when a Pivot is a good idea.

Bigger Pain Point Pivot

This is when your customer appreciates what you are doing to some extent, but tells you about a far more pressing problem they have. This more pressing problem is a bigger Pain Point and something they need fixing quickly and they are prepared to invest in a solution.

In this scenario if you see that this is something you can Pivot towards and serve the customer, then do so. Readjust your offering to meet this need and relaunch as a MVP again.

Different Customer Pivot

Here you discover, despite earlier research you find that the customer Avatar you set out to serve is in fact not as receptive as a different customer type. This second type is far more interested in what you are offering and prepared to buy from you. In this situation again, modify your "Bankable Assumption," Avatar and Pain Point and start to directly target the new group. See if you can achieve your financial objective.

Product Feature Pivot

In this scenario you discover that a specific element of your product or service is of far greater interest to the customer than you realised. If this is the case then detach from your original thinking and go back to the customer with greater emphasis on the feature they like. See how they react to this pivot.

A word to each of the Mind Sets

Idols – be prepared to change, do not let your emotional attachment block out market feedback.

Tsunamis – do not keep pivoting on small changes; ensure there is a value in pivoting rather than pulling out.

Deserts – you do have backup ideas and only pivot if you really see something worthwhile to go for.

Runaways – like Idols be prepared to pull the plug, but if you see a different opportunity explore, explore, explore!

9.10 What you have learned in this Chapter

Although you have previously tested your idea for soundness the ultimate test is in the market. You have learnt a safer, yet expandable product launch process - Minimum Viable Product (MVP). This sits between testing and full roll out. It gives an opportunity to be sure of success and a real-life launch AS WELL AS the opportunity to retreat/rethink without blowing all your money.

Now you are going for a final stage of testing where you are selling in earnest. To summarise the learning:-

- You launch a MVP version of your product or service at minimal costs. A "Good Enough" product.
- You only offer a product or service ethically that you can deliver in some way to the quality promised.
- You will have a ramp up plan ready to roll if the product tests well.
- If the product tests well you go for a rapid ramp up with all your effort.
- If the product does not achieve sales within 30 days, you either, make an objective Pivot Point modification and try again for a further 30 days OR you pull the idea completely and go back for a rethink.
- You do not spend money you do not have on this process.
- You do not spend more than 90 days developing the idea prior to launch.
- If your idea lifts off you will need to have a series of resources and plans ready.

I have also provided a Q&A resource in this Chapter for commonly asked questions about SUSS MVP launches.

In the next Chapter which I recommend you read collectively with this and Chapter 11, you will learn about having the right Mind Set and resources behind your Test Launch.

10 SUSS Your Minimum Viable Product Mind Set

10.1 What You Are Going to Learn in This Chapter

You know your Pain Point and your Test Market. Now it is time to roll out with the right Mental Approach.

Remember the most important objective of your launch is to check whether or not customer prospects in your target market will actually buy from you. To be even more specific – will they put money into your bank account for the product you are currently offering?

At the end of this period you will be making one of 3 decisions.

1. Ramp Up
2. Pivot
3. Drop

Ramp Up - There are 3 scenarios where you can decide to carry on and ramp the business up. They are all based around you having sold successfully against the target you set yourself in the business model stage.

1. You reached your financial target to the original customer type and Pain Point planned.
2. You reached financial target to the original customer type but different Pain Point than planned.
3. You reached financial target to the Pain Point planned but a different customer type.

Pivot – you did not reach your financial target but prospects gave a clear and consistent message that if you made a specific change (not price point) they would buy from you. If you are getting very clear direction from the market on this, do not wait until the end of the 90 days, make the change and Pivot.

You may find your first Pivot gets you closer, but not all the way to gaining sales. If this is the case do not hesitate to Pivot again. Success is often about multiple small changes.

Drop – you did not reach your specific financial target, prospects were **not** prepared to invest in your Pain Point solution and gave no consistent or clear direction on an alternatives worth pivoting on to. It is essential that you listen for clear and consistent market direction, if it is not there do not carry on. If you are in doubt get a second opinion.

It is a very exciting time for you. Enjoy it.

Keep these 6 pieces of A.D.V.I.C.E. in mind for your Roll Out then you will be fine.

They are:-

A is for Accounting – stay in control of your numbers

D is for Discovery – make sure your product/service is discoverable by many customers

V is for Voices– avoid voices of doom inside your head and in your world

I is for Intensity - use your limited time to best advantage

C is for Closing –sales action is vital, close sales and work hard of selling to payment

E is for Energy – maintain your routine, health and diet for maximum energy

10.2. Becoming an Accountant

A good tip for start ups is to make yourself a better accountant than your accountant. This gives you huge advantages in terms of:-

- Profitability
- Tax liability
- Self confidence
- Reduced accounting bills

Get or make a calendar - showing the key tax return, VAT or other accounting requirements in your country. Then mark in your own annual return dates, VAT periods, and so on. Be humble, even if you have previously run a business for 20 years; make sure you get this right.

Watch the budget - Every year – sometimes more often, your government minister will announce changes to tax and tax regulations in your country. Make sure you watch this and read a good review in the followings days. It is worth buying and keeping a quality newspaper the day after any budget.

Leaving until last minute - This is definitely the most common issue. Leave alone, leave alone, leave alone PANIC! Do a little every day. Set an afternoon aside each week just for accounting.

TAD's Traditional Accounting Documents – these are the Balance Sheet, Profit and Loss Account, Cash Flow Forecast, VAT and Tax Return. Learn them; it will take about 10 hours of study to get a basic grip. I have never met an accountant prepared to educate clients on them, so best do it yourself.

Using software – Once you understand the Traditional Accounting Documents or TAD's go onto electronic software. But I strongly recommend you learn your craft on paper first. There are huge advantages in using software BUT ONLY IF YOU UNDERSTAND IT. Understanding is more important than speed early on.

Buy software which suits the size of your business. Buying software which is too big for your business can cause huge problems so go small to start with. Also you may not have to buy accounting software at all in future. New banking apps are now emerging which have built in accounting software within your online app. Some of the leading accounting software providers are working with banks more and more. So buy wisely.

Receipt snaps – one of the great advances in accounting is the ability to take a photograph of a receipt or bill on your smart phone and pull it into your accounting package. Those lost receipts for £2.99 or €5.97 or just $0.99 all add up. So keep it tight and use receipt snapper and snap the receipt as soon as you pay. If you can categorise your items as you go – this is even better.

Be fastidious in retaining purchase receipts as you go – Keep receipts in one place and on your accounting afternoon gather all your loose receipts from your car, van dash board, wallet, gym bag, purse, attaché case or tool bench. Make sure you scoop them all up weekly. Be fastidious. Trying to back track and work out your year's business costs is horrible. You will also pay more tax than you should do. Keep a close record of every penny your business spends.

Having a separate bank account – Be streetwise when it comes to bank charges during your test launch. Get a business account deal that is free for the first year. But if money is very tight, using your personal account for 90 days is an option. Your bank may not like it, but it is a viable method. Working private and business affairs off a single free personal account can be moderately difficult especially when it comes to your tax return. However if you are a sole trader, there is no reason why you should not have two personal bank accounts with different banks. This saves you bank charges in your early days.

If you mix your business and personal finances, long term, you will make life more difficult and actually probably lose tax deductible items along the way. But short term it is ok. Remember always avoid bank charges.

Not filing bank statements in order - It sounds simple, but you'd be amazed how many people don't do it. I am not just talking about paper statements. What happens? You give your statements to your accountant at year-end and they phone back later to tell you a statement is missing.

This means you've just paid your accountant (who probably charges by the hour), to organise your bank statements, when you could have saved money by doing it yourself. Keep the statements for several years. You are likely to need them. Better still download them monthly as a .CSV file.

Organised filing - Be proud of your filing system and organisation. Make it digital. File in date order. Scan like the wind and save to the Cloud for added security. Split invoices into paid and not paid purchase invoices.

Have a distinct place and files for your business - Ideally have a dedicated office if you work at home – even if it is a Harry Potter office under the stairs. There are some great ideas for small offices on Pinterest.

There is something about "going to work" even if you are at your home.

10.3. Discovery

Discovery by prospective customers is the key to selling your product or service. You have to get your message out to enough potential customers and be discovered. Obvious but true.

To launch a successful start up you **HAVE** to be digitally savvy. You have to be. The idea there are digital businesses and non-digital business is now a myth. All entrepreneurs need digital marketing skills. But happily most people are now pretty skilled in terms of website building, social media use and even personal branding. This does not mean you have to do all the work, but you must understand it. Everyone reading this will have different levels of skill, so setting down a uniform approach is not practical. But I have set out what I think to be the essentials in the following Chapter.

Own your digital presence - Do not find anyone to act as your DIGITAL CRUTCH. By being confident with hosting, building a website, e-commerce, understanding SEO and even analytics you can really progress your start up. You <u>have</u> to understand it. As a minimum you must have total control of your

- URL Ownership
- Web space Access
- Email account
- Other Social Media Accounts and Names

Using an agency - I would only recommend using an agency ONCE you understand digital AND can afford SUSTAINED SERVICE. Whether you use your own employees or an agency later on you must always:-

- Own
- Understand
- Be Able to Shut Out Poorly Performing, Rogue Staff or Agencies

However if you have **strong** recommendations from people you trust you can sub-contract digital activity to a 3rd party agency. This can decrease your work load allowing you to focus on selling AND the agency can really help move your discoverability, brand quality and customer service forward. But your launch must succeed in 90 days, so no long term marketing strategies from the agency. Only commit to the launch period. There are of course strategies which take more than 90 days to be effective. But bluntly, this does not help you to sell and assess your idea in a MVP launch, so keep the agency focused on the launch, with the incentive of more work if they deliver.

It's getting easier – thankfully discovery is getting easier for start ups. Some examples include:-

- Piggy backing well known distribution channels is cheap and quick
- You can be discovered and sell on Amazon, eBay and more and more marketplaces
- Facebook advertising is very effective and targeting increasingly precise
- Instagram allows you to earn as an influencer
- YouTube is highly effective if you have discovered a real Pain Point.
- SEO is getting easier thanks to businesses like Yoast.com
- Building websites is also getting easier and template driven
- Websites building tools are improving all the time
- Graphic design tools like the amazing Canva allows you to do much of your own design quickly and with style

Education – No one is fully up to speed on digital marketing – every honest marketer will tell you they are constantly doing courses to improve their knowledge. Digital software and strategy education is now widely available, cheap and sometimes free. This investment in your own skills is vital. I believe the entrepreneur who can use WordPress is far less likely to be taken for a ride by a web-designer, digital agency or member of staff.

Video- video is extremely important in marketing. Educate yourself in video production and get camera savvy. You cannot really avoid it with all social media moving in this direction. Smartphones are amazing but top performers go up a level.

Software – At this stage, your mission is to test launch your business NOT to learn software. This is a controversial view, yet one I hold deeply. When you are running your Test Launch you need the focus to be on discovery and sales. I have seen too many start ups heavily bogged down in learning complex software during their SUSS and before they know it, their launch period is over and they have not even started selling.

So look at what software you absolutely must have. I would be very careful about committing to a full blown Customer Relationship Management (CRM) platform during a test launch. Why? Because they ARE complex! If you have used a CRM application extensively before, then use it. But during test launch I would keep your software to essentials. You will not find out if any major piece of software is right for your long term business from a 7 or 14 day trial. FACT! Be very cautious

In fact for selling I personally would stay with basic software you know, or even Excel, Outlook, Notepad and pen approach until I secured my first clients. Obviously if you have an online store with many products this is different as you will need your website to be a shop with e-commerce capability. But everything needs to stay light.

But typically longer term you will need some or maybe all of the following resources and skills?

- CRM (Customer Relationship Management) or spreadsheet for customer records
- Campaign Tool
- Social Media Sites
- Social Media Feed Aggregator
- Website
- SEO
- E commerce

- E Commerce to Accounting software link
- Graphic design tool
- Video explainer
- Channel integration mobile/voice/online
- Apps for numerous little tasks e.g., currency exchange rates, translation, diary

I emphasise SOME. You have to balance the time, scale and expense of your new venture against your product type, market and need.

Not All Discovery Comes From Proactive Online Marketing - Your business will only grow offline and online if you can get the message to spread. Your online presence may just be about helping people to find you and promotions may need to be physical.

Some useful ways for you to think about being Discovered

Swag- merchandising is a great way to spread your message. I once sent 200 contacts a small Lindt chocolate rabbit for Easter. It was amazingly successful, with so many lovely thank you letters. I had sent multiple emails, with little progress, but the rabbits were amazing. I did get one letter back from a Director of a large bank saying her had shared it with all his staff (2000 +) which made me laugh out loud. The bank of the loaves and fishes I think. Only one individual returned the rabbit saying it was against company policy to accept gifts. So swag worked for me.

Point of sale print materials are now less expensive than ever and Vistaprint have democratised printing for the small business. You can start with very small quantities of diverse items and make your brand and business look much bigger than you are.

What You Must Do - Although not all discovery comes from proactive online marketing, you will always need:-

- A professional online presence
- A means for people to learn about your story
- A means to allow your story to spread
- A manageable level of discovery marketing work
- An affordable level of discovery marketing work

Appropriate Digital Channels for Discoverability

There are still people around the world who make businesses work without spending 90% of their time online AND it is important to say this. Some start ups are purely online business models, of course, selling software and digital training for example.

But the small coffee shop chain needs to make customers feel loved at each of their locations.

Their initial growth should be built on getting their message to spread with a Happy Customers – Come Back Regularly – Tell Their Friends – More Customers mentality. Printable incentives, loyalty cards and events are still valid in this type of business.

Whilst the software company selling to SME's needs super SEO to breakthrough competition and reach their intended market; the engineering company needs a more physical method, to equip their distribution network with maximum technical and demonstration support.

The key point is that not all businesses are based on online models. So their Discoverability needs are going to be different.

Hospitality is a good example of course.

The very successful Brunning and Price gastro pub chain extending throughout the UK had a competent by very small web presence. But word of mouth spread because of the chain's great interiors and nice atmospheres. But managers and servers who clearly were a cut above the normal pub leadership adding to the feeling of quality. This is what made this chain successful. – This led to word of mouth based growth without a doubt.

Engineering is another

Bladon Jets make an electricity generator that can power villages without the need for mains electricity. It is amazing for isolated communities in many countries. Especially useful where power is needed to power cellular networks. The use of a very small jet engine with much lower running and maintenance costs than a typical diesel generator makes this a really interesting product. By partnering with local distributors who already know the market this great technology will realise it's potential. Of course it needs to be demonstrable online. But discoverability to distributors was best achieved by traditional proactive sales contact. Bladon would not be able to reach civic leaders in isolated communities, but local distributors were already servicing their needs.

There is in fact a Spectrum of Discoverability

The Spectrum of Discoverability		
Coffee Shop Chain	**Engineering Business**	**Software Vendor**
Serving Local City or Town Catchments (Chain)	Selling Specialist Higher Value or B2B Products Online	Selling Digital Service Online
You will need a friendly, local-feel and compact online presence replicated as your chain builds	You will need to demonstrate your product and support your distribution channels	You will be fighting for top position on the search engines and SEO will be critical to your success
Discoverability achieved by – High footfall physical location – bring a friend campaign – loyalty campaigns – local community events – local micro sponsorship	*Discoverability achieved by –* Specialist selling based on identifying local distributors i.e. indirect sales. Modest promotional website with strong product demonstration	*Discoverability achieved by –* Hard core SEO success in competitive space. Analytics of advertising and online placement in Google AdWords, PPC for example

With these examples I hope to have demonstrated the point that not every business needs the same channels OR in fact the same coverage.

What I am seeking start ups to avoid is the founder spending 90 days 24/7 online trying to crack open online sales when there are different opportunities to achieve discoverability.

10.4. Voices of Doom and the Minefield of Expert Opinion

There is no consistency in terms of expert advice on business and especially digital marketing strategies for the small business owner. None! There are thousands of experts online offering solutions for passive income.

The truth is like anything else in life, there are no quick fixes and you get out what you put in. I always respect successful people and recommend you do the same. But be careful of

- Software for the start-up to buy which mandates the purchase of further software
- Large advertising giants whose methods can work for HugeCorp with huge budgets but really do not work for limited cash start ups
- Start-ups whose products fit the geographical/business type categories of social media advertising platforms
- Software which you must buy with expensive training to use properly

False Coaches - Once your business starts to fire and sales start to flow, be sure experts will come out of every corner. Do not be seduced by them. Stick to your 90 day MVP launch. You do not need alternative business models.

Learn this process well, stay in control. It is an experience you can repeat in future ventures.

If anyone approaches you to discuss selling or investing in your business before you reach you 3 month goals, give them the following challenge. This was great advice given to me by a senior in Coutts Bank

"Ask your potential investor or buyer to write down a number on a cheque or even piece of paper as their bid for your company and bring it with them. If they cannot do that, they are not senior or serious enough and are just wasting your time."

Remember most of the coaching you will hear will emanate from three main sources:-

- Hugecorp who operate on an entirely different model from you
- Government agencies who exist for political not commercial masters
- People who want to sell you their way of doing things

Good sales gives you control - Do remember one key fact

IF YOU HAVE SALES EVERYTHING ELSE IS JUST SOLID WORK

IF SALES ARE GOOD BUSINESS IS STRAIGHTFORWARD

Now I hear some say "Yes but how long will the business be solid is there are underlying problems being propped up by good sales."

Well I would argue there are many, many very large companies who do many things badly, but are thriving, especially if their market is in rapid growth.

The fact of the matter is this, if a business has strong revenue flow, the rest of it is just WORK.

Making the product, delivering the service, running the office, saying thank you to customers, researching customer feedback, accounts, recruitment, book-keeping and recruitment is just hard work.

It is all just work. Albeit work that should be done professionally, diligently and with enthusiasm.

Problems rise when revenue falls – So long as you have sales revenue coming in and your business model is sound in terms of reasonable longevity and profitability, then you can:-

- Pay your suppliers
- Pay your staff
- Order that machine
- Get that salon fit out
- Refurbish that old bar
- Buy the CRM software

So do not listen to that Voice of Doom – not from anyone!

10.5. Be Intense

At start up you need to be Intense. This is a very different approach to working 9-5. It is unlikely you will be able to do a 37 hour working week during your Test Launch. I suggest a different approach to managing your time, a balance between very hard work and effectiveness. Intensity comes with ruthless attention management, more than excessive working hours.

Ruthless Attention Management

A. You are going to decide to be ruthless in what you allow your attention to dwell on

B. And you are going to mindfully manage your attention

C. You are not going to let the Time Bandits steal your time

Why?

In recent years managing your time has become very difficult indeed. In fact it has become incredibly stressful. Distractions come from every corner, every device demanding attention and the volume of information coming towards ever increasing.

You can only get the intensity you need by having ruthless attention management. When you need to have close attention to your work, you must ruthless defend you time, this needs management. Be civil to those around you, explain that key times are very important to you and you need to defend your time.

It does not seem to matter how much time you have, how far you extend your day, managing time is **such** a challenge. You are under attack from information overload 24 hours a day.

Many failed entrepreneurs report that no matter how hard they tried, getting control of "time" was a huge challenge. *"I spent too long working on the wrong things"* is such a common from "Failed" Entrepreneurs.

Keeping your focus, maintaining a healthy focus on your own goals – not anyone else's! Is the key skill needed to ensure our own success in our commercial ventures and life outside work?

There are two types of attention – attention to your own goals (positive attention) and attention to other peoples' goals/issues/demands (negative attention). – The former represents success, the latter failure.

Some people describe this as vibration. But it must be true that you have a much higher chance to achieve your own business success, if you we focus intensively on it and exclude distractions that things that do not serve you well.

Watch yourself mindfully - Be mindful of your attention. Study and watch yourself on where and how you are directing your attention. If you let it your attention roam free, it will run wild and go in any direction it chooses.

Be very Intense about Your Time – You are starting a new venture to become successful. Right? When you are making progress against our own plans we feel really good and fulfilled. Time is the most valuable commodity for the hard working entrepreneur. Be intense about your time. It feels best is when you are moving forward, doing what you planned. Ruthlessly hold to your plan.

Don't play the defensive game – Too many start ups STILL spend too much time playing the defensive game. Responding to other people's contact, social media, 24/7 news feed and many, many attempts to sell things to our business we do not need. Your time is for your business goals. Serving your clients!

Have a default statement for saying no - You have to keep your commitments tight. If you do not, you will water down your focus on your own goals. Say NO to the Time Bandits.

I recommend you develop a stock phrase or way to say no. Plan a way of saying no

- In person
- In social media
- On the phone
- In email

Do not offer advice, time or resources for Free – Do not squander any of these limited resources. Respect their value yourself. If you do not, no-one else will.

Don't respond to guilt - Finally, some people around you will use guilt as a weapon when you say no. Do not allow yourself to feel guilty for saying no.

Recovering intense concentration - Once your attention is distracted a single time, one tends to find it is not a single shot, but many, like a distraction machine gun!

So once you see that first attention stealer, do EVERYTHING to stop it dead as soon as possible and prevent the machine gun filling your attention with holes.

Have a "default" positive to quickly switch your attention to. Since distractions quickly occupy our mind. I have my intense concentration music collection I switch on, including Solfeggio frequencies. You can find lots of it on YouTube for free. I really recommend Solfeggio music for improving attention intensity and span.

If you play the theme to Rocky or something more contemporary (what can I say I love Rocky and I am middle aged!) to help you in the gym or running you will understand the motivational effects of music.

Whatever your taste in music, when you feel you are losing your intensity tunes always improves focus.

Know when to take a break – We all need to know when to take a break. Sometimes when you are fatigued you can spend hours trying to complete a task. You expect it to take an hour but three hours later the end is not in sight. The return on your time investment is poor. You have to know when to stop and give it another try later. Simply pouring more and more energy in at that point will drain, frustrate and demotivate you.

Stop – go on to something else. Think! Your attention is valuable. The most valuable thing you have in fact.

Your success will require more than mindless hard work. You will hit unexpected barriers. You will certainly have to find ways of moving forward without money.

To do this you are going to need creative problem solving. This type of process only comes when you are relaxed and can think straight. By taking yourself out of the business process and social media distractions, you can get past barriers and come up with new ideas to move forward.

Often the best ideas come along at the strangest times. Walking the dog, pushing the kids on the swings, in a dream, watching a movie, on a beach in Spain.

Time off is essential to maintain creative thought energy

Not all your work has to be at a desk or workbench - Why not do daily planning reviews while you exercise. I often run a Planning Review through my head as I train in the swimming pool!

Professional entrepreneurs know their plans intimately. It will be fixed in your mind like a tattoo. So take time daily to review it and the main goals you are working towards. It does not have to be at your desk. Review your plan while swimming in the pool (I do) or jogging or walking the dog. I find this gives me the best ideas and clarity. I can focus whilst swimming on the plan, challenges and potential solutions.

10.6. What exactly is Closing?

Closing is gaining definite and mutually understood agreement on an exchange of product or services for payment within an agreed timeframe.

Closing is Critical

I have seen several very good MVP test launches fail because of poor closing. It is a key skill, which does not come naturally to many people. But, it can be learned quickly and effectively.

Sometimes entrepreneurs get everything right, but closing. The fear is that the prospective customer will say "No" to buying from you. But all good sales coaches will tell you that a "No" is a good thing. Here's why:-

1. You get to hear their objection (it may be a misunderstanding, something you can address OR you establish they are definitely not going to buy and put your time/effort into another prospect).
2. You can get a list of objections from one client. They may offer several reasons, which you can record and then deal with the most important one. It's normally not the first one they say!
3. If you see consistent objections from lots of people it may be something you can fix with a pivot.
4. They may say "No" but mean "Yes" but want a better deal, which you can address with negotiation. But do not cave in on your pricing! There may be a small concession you can offer to close the business

Good Closing Habits

- Always Be Closing ABC
- Do not be afraid of hearing "No"
- Ask for the business early in the conversation
- Ask repeatedly for their business
- Record their objections carefully
- Ask them to repeat or clarify their objections
- Do not assume price is the main objection – even if they say it is
- Make a list of likely objections and ways you can counter them
- Practice closing with friends, relatives or even better a professional sales person or buyer

10.7. Energy is Key

During your MVP launch you will be busy. You will also have disappointments. This is certain.

You need to maintain your personal energy and motivation.

Here are my top 15 tips for maintaining your energy

1. Have a selling routine – not a marketing routine. Set aside time purely for closing deals and selling. This will keep your energy high.
2. Always back yourself and your own decision making
3. Get up early 5AM – this gives you 2-3 hours clean working time before the world comes to life, the kids wake up, the phone starts ringing and distractions start to hit you.
4. Sleep at least 7 hours – you do not build successful businesses by getting ill from fatigue.
5. Surround yourself with supporters - Keep away from negative people
6. Exercise – keep moving even if you are working from a desk. For example put a cycling machine near your desk and jump on it for 5 minutes every hour. Do your own thing but stay fit.
7. Eat well – you know it makes sense.
8. Be grateful for every little bit of progress
9. Celebrate all successes no matter how small
10. Learn from things that go wrong, and then let them go. Don't let anything haunt you
11. Work very hard, give your idea every chance of success
12. Avoid distractions – keep social social media (that is not a typo) for after work
13. Follow successful positive people
14. Do not become too isolated from society during this period.
15. Remember you are helping clients overcome problems. This is a great motivator and source of energy.

10.8 What you have learned in this Chapter

In this Chapter you have heard the importance of having the right Mind Set for your SUSS Test Launch.

- Go
- Pivot
- Drop

As a Professional Entrepreneur you know all of these outcomes equal a success if reached within 90 days.

You have learned that selling and closing are vital skills you must learn in order to succeed.

I have also introduced the ADVICE learning to help you stay focused and positive on a range of issues affecting the success of your launch.

In the next Chapter which I recommend you read as Chapters 9,10 and 11, you will learn about effective SUSS Sales and Marketing techniques that you can employ during your SUSS Test Launch and beyond.

11. SUSS Minimum Viable Product Effective Sales and Marketing

11.1 What You Are Going to Learn in This Chapter

In this Chapter Start Up Safe Sequence (SUSS) I will show how to simplify your sales and marketing down to core activities that align with the minimum viable product approach.

You will be better placed to do this by stripping out several marketing concepts, which although valid for established businesses, will not help you in the MVP launch.

The main learning is what are the key sales and marketing actions to support an effective launch.

11.2. Selling is the Primary Objective

Remember, the MVP launch is to prove you can sell to your discovered Pain Point at the price you established in business planning.

This is true whether you are selling in a traditional way face to face with customers, in a retail store environment, online with your own ecommerce store or using Amazon/eBay type channels.

11.3 No Need for the 7P's of Promotion – 3 are Simpler

Many marketing advisors will start you off with the 7P's of Marketing – I don't because you already know what Product, Price, Positioning, People are from your earlier work.

- Product – you know exactly what your product (or rather Pain Point solution is already)
- Price – your planning research has assessed and led you to your price points for launch
- **Promotion** – we do not have this right now
- **Packaging** – this will need work and extends beyond wrapping
- Positioning – we are totally clear on this through our earlier work
- People – we know who our partners are and at this stage we are not building a team

So going forward we can really say that at this stage in the SUSS the three key items you need absolutely clarity on are Sales, Promotion, Packaging:-

Sales - This is you being able to gain payment from customers on your existing product at the price you predetermined during business planning.

Promotion - Remember you have already defined your audience really well. You know you are working to solve a specific Pain Point with a specific group of prospective customers. You must develop a tight message conveying INTENT to solve the customer's Pain Point, in ALL your sales and marketing work.

Packaging Packaging is not just the paper box on your product. It is your website, social media presence and of course YOU, your personal brand. But like everything at the MVP stage, packaging needs to be simple, cost effective yet acceptable to your customer in terms of quality and trust.

11.4 Top 10 considerations in choosing your Launch Sales and Marketing plan

Think about these key considerations when setting up your plan.

Where your customer listens – The first and MOST /IMPORTANT consideration when choosing your promotional strategy is where and how the customer listens. You spent time and effort in the market research stage asking what your customer listens to. These are the channels you need to get into. If it is Facebook be on Facebook, if it is your local market put up a pop-up store there.

Marketing budget – Your marketing budget is key to everything. It dictates which channels are open to you. If you cannot afford them, do not use them! It is possible with work to launch with virtually no money, thanks to digital resources. So do not be discouraged if you do not have too much money.

Proximity of customer – This is often not fully considered when planning launches. Personal selling to customers a long way from home is very expensive and will soon drain a private citizen of their savings. Think about this carefully. Consider the use of video conferencing. I am using the excellent Zoom for personal selling and it really serves me well. It can also be used for webinar promotions. Closer to home if you are marketing to local customers then posters, brochure stands and other physical marketing material will be useful, especially if synchronised with social media.

Branded or unbranded product – Do consider branding, but do not be slave to it. You can refine it later. Ensure you align to a customer Pain Point. So do not go too far or invest too much in branding at this point. If you have a moment of branding genius good for you and Go for It!

Your own or distributed product – If you are distributing a product for a third party, consider using marketing and brand materials from their site. You can request a logo pack and base design files in Adobe /illustrator or an alternative that suits you both. This can save lots of time as well as copywriting and design costs.

Seasonality – Please consider seasonality. Your promotions have to synchronise with the buying season. In fashion awareness of buying lead times is critical. Do not get this wrong.

Purchase frequency – Consider, your type of customer carefully. Generally online and physical advertising is used for fast moving consumer goods (FMCG). In industrial consumables there are big and small clients of course. Personal selling may be essential to win large customers, but the cost of travel, and overnight stays can be very substantial. Smaller clients are best served by ecommerce.

Margin per sale – Deciding which tools to use is best determined by the achievable margin per sale. If this is a matter of pennies, then low cost, widely spread promotions will be the key. But if a single deal can bring in thousands of dollars than more personal marketing and selling tools are needed.

Buying norms Many (yet not all) major organisations are not open to speculative sales. Knocking at the reception of a major city law firm and asking to meet a partner will be unlikely to succeed and may cause lasting damage to your ability to sell to that firm. Consider how your clients want to buy. Sure there is always room for disruptive methods and guile, but respect client preferences.

Competition - At your MVP launch focus on your own service quality. But if you can identify opportunities where you can take customers away from competitors, go for it! This can be a very effective launch strategy worth consideration.

11.5. SUSS Sales and Marketing Launch Sheet Plan

So far in the SUSS sequence you have done a lot of work on your strategy. Now it is time to break that strategy into a clear sales and marketing plan, which is clear, effective and manageable – Bite Sized Chunks. The blank document below is for you to examine and then customise for your own use. It is called the SUSS Sales and Marketing Launch Sheet Plan

Here are the elements of the SUSS Sales and Marketing Launch Sheet Plan. It is made up of 9 elements spread across Getting Leads, Converting Leads and Delighting Clients.

Top of Sheet Reminder

Fill in your Target Customer and your core Pain Point solution message at the top of the SUSS Launch Sheet along with your Bankable Solution. This is a reminder to retain clarity.

Getting Leads

This is about the tools and channels you will use to get your leads

Funnels - the step by step journeys potential customers go through on the way to purchase.

Media – the media upon which you base your sales funnel and other marketing messages

CTA's – Free guides or gifts to call to action (CTA) and get contact details from prospects.

Converting Leads

What you do once the customer has given you contact details to manage the lead, build confidence/familiarity with your service and close for the order and sale. (Money in your bank!)

First Connection Lead – your initial reaction to the customer on receiving their contact details

Confidence Building – steps to increase customer confidence through your funnels/buy into your tribe and what it stands for.

Closing – encouraging the customer to purchase and close the deal to a paid sale.

Delighting Clients

This is about giving new clients an excellent experience of your service, finding out how you can improve and getting referrals from your new clients to aid your marketing and sales work.

Onboarding – making sure once they have paid that the customer is not disappointed. This matters even in the MVP launch. As you know news of poor service travels very fast.

Feedback – understanding what customers liked and didn't like and using this information to improve your offering.

Referrals – gaining referrals is critical to the new start up. It really is. You need a plan to encourage customers to give you referrals as soon as possible after purchase.

SAFER STARTUP SEQUENCE LAUNCH SHEET

	Market	Pain Point	Bankable Solution
GETTING	FUNNELS	MEDIA	CALL TO ACTION
CONVERTING	1ST CONNECTION	CONFIDENCE	CLOSING
DELIGHTING	ONBOARDING	FEEDBACK	REFERRALS

11.6. Example SUSS Launch Sheet

The example we are going to use to further develop your understanding of the SSUP Launch Sheet is a Green Pain Point. This is when customers have to throw things away when trying to be green.

This example relates to plastic razors, which people like me are finding increasingly hard to justify.

<u>Market</u> – Environmentally conscious men with sons.

<u>Pain Point</u> – Having to throw away plastic razors that end up polluting the sea and planet

<u>Bankable Solution</u> – Providing leadership on transition to more sustainable shaving and the provision of a shaving conversion kit. This kit is made up of environmentally friendly items including a steel lifetime razor, shaving soap and brush plus recyclable blades. "Plastic Free Shaving!"

11.7. Getting Leads

11.7.1. Funnels

Sales funnels are marketing pathways set out to map our routes customers can take to find, consider and buy from you. They are constantly evolving. Some web research will quickly show you which are suitable for your business. I would suggest at MVP launch you need a minimum of 5 fully operational funnels with reporting. Ideally more! But you have to be able to manage them consistently well.

For each funnel you have map out every stage of the customer's journey. Identify which software and other needs you have and use this as your plan.

There are many lead funnels and innovations every day. Here are some digital and non-digital examples:-

Squeeze Page Funnel – you want the visitors email address! That is the goal of this simple normally two page funnel. Brutal simplicity is important here with no frills pages. A question that really arouses curiosity is the key here. The visitor has to provide their email address in order to receive the answer to their question. Raising curiosity to get visitors to opt-in is the objective. Later I give you a fuller explanation of the Pain Point solution. This is the ideal funnel for the MVP start up.

The Reverse Squeeze Page Funnel – this method reverses the Squeeze Page Funnel by showing all the details about (for example) Plastic Free Shaving and what it stands for and the damage it seeks to prevent to the environment. It is best delivered with video. At the end of the presentation the prospect is asked to sign up. Although conversion rates are normally lower than a Squeeze Page Funnel, quality of the leads are often much better. Plus your Thank You page at the end of the funnel allows you to encourage sharing with friends AND to impart more detailed information.

Survey Funnel – a survey about shaving, attitudes to the environment and shavers in the respondents' family helps build rapport with your respondent and shows you which type of customer they are. This allows different promotions for example "Dad to Son First Shave Kit Gift" for fathers with teenage sons or Teenagers concerned about the planet. Plus you can capture their critical email address.

Video Sales Letter Funnel – this is simply a video selling your product or service. At the end of the video the price is announced and a payment button appears. In our example it would be to order the Plastic Free Shaving kit.

The Lead Magnet Funnel – you offer a freebie to the customer in exchange for their email address. This is commonly a guide, mini course or video. The main thing it is real value and not just a sales brochure. In the case of the Shave Kit it could be a calculator showing how many razors the visitor will throw away during the rest of their life.

Public relations as a Funnel – PR is still a very effective lead generator. The environment media would be receptive to articles and stories about green shaving. Our razor example could be packaged as the "Plastic Free Shave" campaign, with PR articles going out to publications, newspapers and TV/Radio. Prospects will find you online as a funnel entry point.

Influencer Funnels – this is an effective way of getting leads and is a funnel in its own right. You may not be able to afford an A-list celebrity, but environment-conscious influencers do promote for free.

Event Funnels – for example an environmental support gig or festival. In the Plastic Free Shaving example the funnel start point may be a physical stand demonstrating your Pain Point and solution.

Print Advertising – there is still a place for this. For example an advert in the EasyJet flight magazine could bring in significant lead numbers. Print media still has a role to play and it is not too expensive.

Your Task: Identify your top 5 funnels. Name them and write down on your SUSS Launch Sheet. Also draw a flow chart showing how each funnel will work. One sheet per funnel.

11.7.2. Media

Once you have selected your funnels, mapping them out makes your media choices very clear.

Before we look at some examples about media I would like to revisit your Customer Relationship Management (CRM) options and provide a word of warning.

Because your prime concern in the MVP Roll Out is getting sales, the time you put into working your CRM **must** be manageable. Free software trials are tempting. But most people will not learn enough about the software during the trial and thereafter they are stuck learning the software – and paying for it! I actually think a 7 or 14 day trial of CRM software is a joke and seriously impacts on MVP success. Too much time perfecting understanding of a CRM system can wreck a MVP launch.

So my advice is to think about your personal skills with CRM software and to act in the following way during test launch (what you do afterwards is a different matter!).

1. **You are very familiar with a particular CRM System** - use it in the MVP launch for funnel management, lead capture and metrics.
2. **You're not especially CRM savvy but good in IT generally** – use a simple system like Microsoft Office 365 Outlook Customer Manager which comes free with Office 365.
3. **You are not good on IT** – use a MS Excel spreadsheet for the first 90 days. Or if you are not using digital funnels so much, use a lead pad. Basic I know, but the core goal is to test if you can sell your product or service, not to spend 90 days learning how to use a software application.

Using Media in Getting Leads

Funnel	Media/Tools Needed	Feeding Into
Squeeze Page	Basic webpage or Facebook/Twitter/LinkedIn to webpage email capture	Lead Capture CRM or organised spreadsheet
Reverse Squeeze Page	Video presentation, explainer to call to action + email capture.	Lead Capture CRM or organised spreadsheet
Survey	Web page to survey tool link (Survey Monkey/Survey Gizmo). This can be issued across multiple channels including Face Book Page, Linked In and Instagram (if it goes direct to your profile URL). You can also embed the code into your website should you wish.	Lead Capture CRM or organised spreadsheet
Video Sales Letter	You will need to produce a video promotion. You can spend a lot or a little on videos. Low cost cartoon video creators and template based stills to video tools are available. The key is to be authentic and focus on the Pain Point and your solution. Investment in quality on your videos is recommended.	Lead Capture CRM or organised spreadsheet
Lead Magnet	Lead magnets come in various forms. Typically they are digital from your website or Facebook page a free PDF guide or video, it can be a physical gift, or even free tickets to a webinar or live event.	Lead Capture CRM or organised spreadsheet
PR	You will be using PR for lead generation. Your goal is not to pioneer or change public opinion - it is to SELL. Remember journalists like things that haven't been launched yet. So contact them very early. Ensure your business name appears clearly in all articles.	Lead Capture CRM or organised spreadsheet
Print	You need high quality print ready designs, outsource design work to Fiverr.com or use the excellent Canva if you are confident. Choosing print advertising is all about cost per lead and clear evidence that delivers results.	Lead Capture CRM or organised spreadsheet
Influencers	Great in Instagram and Pinterest. If you can get well followed influencers to promote/be seen in your brand you will get interest. But remember Instagram does not allow URL's in posts so you may need your brand to be written on the post image or story.	Lead Capture CRM or organised spreadsheet
Event	Online digital events can be automated using software like Clickfunnels. More locally you can run events promoted on Facebook to gain physical audiences and this does work well.	Lead Capture CRM or organised spreadsheet

11.7.3. Call to Action CTA's

No matter how good your funnel is you have to get your site visitors to give you the action of letting you have their email. This Call To Action or CTA is vitally important. It is also commonly overlooked, as entrepreneurs get excited about the creative design and video production process.

Every funnel must have a Call to Action. CTA's give your audience the opportunity to progress to being a customer or client. Without leads there are no sales.

There is no doubt that CTA's are a science and the wording, button size and placement are very, very important. Here are some top tips of CTA's

1. Frame your CTA – you have the button and surrounding imagery and lead in text.
2. Know your market; something that is terribly overlooked is culture in CTA. North American CTA's do not transfer universally well to European and other markets. They can appear sleazy. By contrast British CTA's can appear to be too polite and not direct enough. Find a balance.
3. CTA's are not just for websites, but email, Instagram, Facebook, plus many others.
4. Do not be dull, you are reliving a Pain Point so be emotive and creative.
5. Make your visitors enthusiastic
6. Emphasis shortage of time
7. Show a strong reason to take action now
8. Create shortage and work on FOMO (Fear of Missing Out)
9. Be aware how your CTA appears on different devices
10. Use numbers when possible, people respond well to numbers
11. Avoid CTA's that threaten or question people's energy or commitment. There is a universal dislike of this type of CTA, which most often lead to the page being closed. "If you're not interested in your child's health do not click" it just sounds both rude and desperate.
12. Strong commands work best with a powerful verb at the beginning of your CTA. It's all about being clear and concise with your CTA. Examples include:-
    - Get Started
    - Create an Account
    - Sign Up Free
    - View Demo
    - Contact Sales
    - Learn More
    - Join Free
    - Shop Now
    - Explore the Collection

11.8. Converting

Now let us deal with converting. Your CTA has provided you with approval and means to reach out to your prospect. The sequence shown on the Sheet covers

- 1st Contact – the first time you communicate after being given permission
- Confidence – building trust and confidence in you and your Pain Point Solution
- Closing – Getting the prospect to spend with you and become a client

You key goal here in your MVP test is to market to your leads until they commit to buying from you and they unsubscribe. Do not be discouraged by people unsubscribing it is a normal part of the sales process.

11.8.1 1st Contact

The whole of your strategy is based around solving the customer's Pain Point. So stick to your strategy throughout. You first contact with the lead should:-

- Show gratitude for sharing their details
- Position yourself as a champion with a solution for their Pain Point problem
- Be pacey, hinting at action
- Provide a clear explanation of the Pain Point and how you really can solve it
- Offer an opportunity to buy, then and there.

11.8.2. Confidence

Of course leads may not immediately buy, so it is important that you steadily build in a sequence of mailers a case for signing up. You are building up a compelling story.

This can include

- Satisfied customer testimonials
- Numbers showing the saving
- More detail on how the solution works
- Live video of customers using the service
- A quiz to further engage the customer in the Pain Point problem
- More depth explanation of the Pain they may be feeling and what will happen if it goes unresolved
- A Q&A showing the top 5 or 10 questions people ask about the product or service
- Your story and why you genuinely want to help

11.8.3. Closing

Remember your SUSS MVP Roll Out is about confirming there is market for your product or service and those customers want to buy it. In the MVP scenario you cannot be taking long drawn out sales cycles. It is essential to be closing business. You are closing business on a specific OFFER.

If you are not closing business, but you are getting registrations, it is likely your offer is not strong enough OR your story is not strong enough.

To be clear, changing an offer or a story is not a pivot. You are tweaking and improving your message to get the business. You are not changing the basis of your MVP.

Do make very sure that your payment methodology is very simple. If it is not, then rip it up and make it simple.

Please do not discount to get the business. You planned your price point carefully and reducing the price is unlikely to give you more sales anyway in this scenario.

Have a closer look at your story in the Confidence section. Is it giving a strong enough Why Buy? Try something else if it is not working.

Perhaps your offer is not good enough. You can always contact some of your leads privately to ask what stopped them buying. They will tell you, believe me and you can change your process and offer from then on.

11.9. Delighting

Now we look at the 3 Delighting phases of the SSUS Launch Sheet – Onboarding, Feedback and Referrals. Last but not least referrals!

11.9.1 Onboarding

Do not be casual about your onboarding process. There is nothing worse than selling that promises great thing and a poor experience or service once you have paid. We have all experienced it and in the social media age we are unforgiving.

POOR ONBOARDING CAN WRECK YOUR MVP LAUNCH

I have just 3 recommendations for great onboarding at this stage of the SUSS.

A. Map the customer's journey with you in advance

Have a flow chart "ONBOARDING MAP" of the customer's journey from day one. Draw it on your office wall or white board. Get very familiar with it.

Every time a customer has a problem, see it as a "Bottleneck" fix it of course, but record it and watch for repeats using the flow chart as your guide.

B. Think "Bottlenecks"

No organisation gets onboarding completely right first time. I used to run a Standard in the contact centre world called Right First Time. What it taught me is that customers really, really hate having to contact you twice or more about a problem. But if you jump on the customer's issue and fix it rapidly, you actually build MORE loyalty than if they had no issues. Yes REALLY. You can even leverage it to get referrals and endorsements.

So if you think about your Onboarding Map, you will start to get repetition of a customer issue at a specific bottleneck, you can change this element of the process to improve service.

But, do not be afraid to tell the world about it, inform that you noticed an issue was recurring and this is what you have done about it.

Bottlenecks are always changing and will move around your map. They can also be prompted to change due to external events – even the weather! But keep on top of the issues and you will succeed.

C. Over-Deliver

Of course you are going to work with customers to drive out problems. But over deliver and Wow your customers with service. Some ideas include:-

- Great personal welcomes
- Give superb training. Check, check and check the customer is happy with it
- Send a handwritten thank you note by post
- Send a small Thank You gift in post
- Be human rather than automated
- Make you receipts/invoices a work of art and personalisation, thanking for their business

11.9.2. Feedback

As a small start-up during your MVP launch, do not run your feedback from customers like HugeCorp. Be personal. Remember you are leading a tribe to change and really help solve a Pain Point. Make your feedback that of a leader in terms of product and the quality of your service.

Avoid at all costs the ubiquitous Net Promoter Score question – ""how likely are you to recommend us on a scale from 0 to 10." That question is as over-used, as it is entirely BORING to your customer. What a yawn!

During the MVP stage gathering feedback should be highly personal and answer:-

- Why customers bought – to check it against your Pain Point concept
- Which demographic did your buyer come from? Were they from the Avatar you expected or elsewhere?
- Why customers didn't buy from you? What change would have prompted them to buy?
- How easy was it for customers to deal with you?
- How well did the payment process work?
- During the MVP launch, if it is manageable you need to gain highly personal feedback from as many customers as possible, even if it involves calling them all.
- Finally always ask for feedback and reward feedback with a little gift.
- Call as many new customers you can and ask if they are happy.

11.9.3. Referrals

The word referral actually covers two different things – Endorsements and Referral Leads. They do overlap, but even though I risk stating the obvious let me set them both out.

Endorsements - Firstly it is getting written (or video) recommendations for your products. For a start-up this is very, very important as you need as many positive "proof-sources" endorsing your service or product as possible. This would extend to encouraging social media sharing.

In a B2B setting you will probably want written referrals and the agreement to put the client's logo on your website OR beef this up into a full testimonial that you can use in online and print materials.

Always work on encouraging happy clients to share their happiness on social media. You can offer a voucher knocking a percentage off their next purchase if they tell others on Facebook, share a photo on Instagram, or tell others about how happy they are on LinkedIn.

As soon as you get a happy customer ask for their help in telling your story. Make them your heroes. Let them tell the world your story. Taking this customer-led approach WILL attract new customers because you will have high credibility. The more you focus on real life buyers personas, their real experience of your product or service and their end to end customer journey the more success you will have.

Referral Leads - Secondly referrals are leads from satisfied customers to other people they know.

A referral programme turns the getting of referral leads into a process. You are going to reward customers by incentives for asking other people they know to try your product or service.

<u>DO NOT UNDER ESTIMATE THE POWER OF REFERRALS</u>

- 88% of marketeers use referral marketing – that really says something about its success.
- A prospect referred by a friend is TWICE as likely to buy from you as referrals from a stranger
- A referral from the same demographic (say single parents) is twice as likely to be effective as a general referral
- 3/4 of B2B marketeers say referrals are "good or excellent quality"
- It is actually cheaper than a new lead from scratch, actually costing less than half as much.

11.10 What you have learned in this Chapter

What you have learnt in this Chapter is a simplified sales and marketing approach optimised for the SUSS Test Launch.

You have examined 9 phases covering Getting, Converting and Delighting clients.

Like every Stage in the SUSS simplicity is the answer.

Of special importance is using referrals from early adopter clients to get more clients.

Plus, ensure you do not over-burden yourself with very complex CRM software. CRM's are important do not get me wrong, but keep it manageable during the MVP stage.

A final word is build your sales and marketing within the resources you have and go for it. Work hard; keep it simple and Always Be Closing.

In the next and final Chapter I offer you some final words of advice and encouragement. Well done for taking the time to Choose an Idea like a Professional Entrepreneur.

12. Final Words and Tips

I have a few final words to you, in the form of my top 10 tips.

1. Don't beat yourself up if you haven't been able to find an idea so far – it's not unusual

2. Finding a Pain Point is more important than just finding an idea

3. Be objective about your ideas, love your partner, spouse or family but not any single idea

4. Make sure you find an opportunity that you can Scale, Repeat and Get Out Of

5. Avoid creating a Job without pension or opportunity to earn big (Create a Business!)

6. Do not rely on any one expert's opinion, get multiple viewpoints

7. Never launch a business before a small scale test

8. Sell hard during your test launch – things don't sell themselves

9. Be prepared to Pivot more than once, but if it fails test launch let it go. Don't flog a dead horse

10. If customers buy, Go, Go, Go, Ramp Up and Go for It!

Finally, my sincere best wishes for great success in Choosing an Idea with Confidence!

Good Judgement

Michael Allen

www.ingramcontent.com/pod-product-compliance
Lightning Source LLC
Chambersburg PA
CBHW072030230526
45466CB00020B/1287